YOUR BEST SHOT

BE THE LEADER OF YOUR LIFE... GOLF SHOWS YOU HOW

JORGE J CRODA

Foreword by
ANTHONY WILLIAMS
Foreword by
KEVIN LONG

Author JORGE J CRODA MORANDO, First edition, February 2021, @2020 Jorge Croda

- www.jorgecroda.com
- contacto@jorgecroda.com
- www.crodaconsulting.com
- crodaconsulting@gmail.com
- https://golf63blog.wordpress.com

- LinkedIn: Jorge J Croda
- Twitter: @jorgecroda
- Facebook: Jorge j Croda
- Instagram: jorgecrodam
- YouTube: crodaconsulting

Colaboration:

- **Proofreading**: Sandra Camacho Verand // LinkedIn: Sandra Camacho Verand
- **Academic Proofreading**: Giovanny Herrera Muñoz // LinkedIn: Giovanny Herrera Muñoz
- **English Editor**: Anthony Williams // LinkedIn: Anthony Williams
- **Publisher**: Inmersión Digital // inmersion.digital
- **Cover Design:** Marca con tu Marca.

ACKNOWLEDGMENTS

Infinite thanks to...

My eternal Father, to God, because looking through his eyes I could see that each blow was only a wake-up call to what is truly important... love!

The love of Linda, my wife, who lives with me this story of constant learning, but most of all, I thank her for sharing with me the unique experience of creating a new life... I think nothing compares to that! ... Being parents changed us forever.

My children, Jimena, María José and Jorge, who took me to another level of love.

My mom Luz Maria and my dad Jorge, without them, plain and simple, I would not be who I am today... I want to tell you that I do not change anything of what I have lived... and I know that my dad is listening to me from heaven.

My siblings Regina and Javier, taught me to take responsibility very early on... and again love came out to meet me and gave me the strength I needed in those moments; and that same love still keeps us united, even though Javier is no longer with us.

My brothers -in-law Abelardo y Lorenia

To my in-laws Juan Manuel and Herlinda, my brothers-in-law Juan Manuel, Sergio, Teresa, Judith y Stu.

From my mother's uncles-in-law, Humberto (Italian) and Ed (American), I learned the values of perseverance, curiosity, creativity and innovation; they gave me the opportunity to experiment with any idea, no matter how crazy or risky it might be. They also taught me to see opportunities, to be authentic, to be myself, not to live by what people will say... and all this from love.

To my nephews Yamile, Ivanna, Abelardo and Javier.

To my grandfather Gabriel for his wise advice, his teachings and his unconditional and infinite love that taught me to feel that I am important... thank you!

To all these people who influenced my life to be the way it is today:

To my teacher Ramón Valdez Castellanos who taught me how to channel my emotions through the arts such as declamation, mandolin and marimba.

Don Juan Cobo, for taking me to learn about golf.

Professional Lucio Méndez, my first golf teacher.

Gary Player, for being my inspiration as a player and as a human being.

Barry Lots, for teaching me the art of being a master golf professional.

J.J. Kegan, for teaching me the fundamentals of the golf business in a comprehensive way.

Tom Schneider and the SEAS golf league for lovingly welcoming me as a friend.

Rafael Barajas for everything I have learned, who has allowed me to have the honor of being a *GCSAA member* for over 14 years.

my friend Carlos Guzman, who took me to meet First Tee and many contacts in FW.

Kevin Long, my friend for everything I have learned, who has allowed me to have the honor of being a *coach* at First Tee for over 10 years.

Richard Best, my friend, for being my inspiration as an organizational *coach*.

Rafael Maratea, my friend and brother, who has always been supportive.

Dr. Luis Gaviria, for his life teachings and training as a neuro coach.

Iñigo Soto, for his friendship and his approach to the European golf market.

Anthony Williams, for your friendship and inspire me to make the green industry GREENER!

To all the organizations in the golf industry in the United States for hosting me and allowing me to educate and grow in this fascinating sport and share my knowledge to grow the game of golf.

And to Sandra Camacho Verand, for accompanying me in this my first book, her collaboration in the style correction, her ideas, advice and research of the topics have been very helpful and, above all, she was always very present, I realized that for her this work is more than that... it is part of her life.

And to Giovanny Herrera for his professional academic review and technical advice on each section of this book. His contributions made this work an excellent resource for the reader, seen from the neuroeducation perspective.

DEDICATION

Because when you think you can't love anymore... a new life is created and love grows and renews itself... on September 23, 2020 Camila came into our lives... my first granddaughter!

This book is for her.

In the following lines I am going to talk about golf, its fundamentals, everything it gives us and teaches us so that we are able to take our lives to a new level of peace and happiness... I feel a very great need -almost imperious-, as well as deep, sincere and honest, to share with you all my experience in this beautiful sport because it is capable of radically changing lives... it did that with mine!

*There is a very interesting concept called "epigenetic inheritance", which is the **transmission of information** from one generation to another. Unfortunately, everything indicates that our traumas and bad experiences are inherited by our children... so, wouldn't it be really important, and even decisive, to reverse our negative* *aspects and experiences, and, on the contrary, perhaps achieve the highest possible quality of life and qualities?*

That is why this book is for you Camila, because beyond how much you can achieve in your life, tuo nonno has reached, thanks to golf, the state of peace and happiness that I have been able to give to your mommy and that I pray to God has reached you and gives you the strength you need to be immensely prosperous and happy on your own.

Never forget that you are not alone and that you are very important... I wish you the life you desire Camila!

FOREWORD

BY ANTHONY L. WILLIAMS

I have known Jorge Croda for many years and we have served together on many Boards and committees representing a cross section of causes and businesses.

The one thing that separates Jorge from others is his vision and drive to see that the vision is realized.

Ultimately he wants to see things improve and in this book, "Your Best Shot" he shares timeless lessons of a life well lived through the simple values within the game of golf. You will soon find the key things that you can do to create your own personal path of success for golf and life.

Jorge and I have traveled together many times. Often we have traveled to grow the game of golf and deliver messages of growth and positivity. Many times we have traveled to Washington DC to participate in activities such as National Golf Day and represent our home State of Texas in meetings with Congressman and other legislators. These meetings are critical as we teach others the environmental, fiscal and personal benefits of golf while welcoming new allies in our search for excellence. Jorge excels in these opportunities as he speaks with a passion and sense of urgency that everyone can understand. The pages of this book reflect the lessons of these journeys as Jorge transports you from course to course and into the very halls of leadership that have shaped our nation.

Jorge practices the methods and skills that he is teaching every day. He tests the value of new thinking and holds the truth of tradition in high value. This allows Jorge even in difficult times such as the recent pandemic to remain positive and take steps toward crafting a better life for himself and others.

He is a masterful coach that invests time and energy into all those he is connected with. His success as a golf course superintendent and player stem from a desire to take action using the best strategies and tools available while improving those around him. He sets a great example and is always learning and making the most of each day.

This will become apparent as you read through the book. Jorge is many things as you will discover. He is a husband, father, friend, superintendent, coach and entrepreneur to name a few but at the core of it all he has a servant's heart and wants to a build legacy of excellence.

I encourage you to take notes as you read the book and reread sections that you find special interest in as this book will remind you to constantly work on improving your game on the links and in life. Jorge is sharing the details of his life's journey in the hope that you can find encouragement and the path to success.

I join with Jorge in thought and prayer wishing each one that reads this book and embraces the call for excellence will find the joy and majesty of a life well lived and a game well played.

Respectfully,

Anthony L. Williams, CGCS, CGM
Director of Golf Course and Landscape Operations
TPC Four Seasons Golf and Sports Club Dallas at Las Colinas
Master Life Coach and 9th Degree Black Belt

FOREWORD
BY KEVIN LONG

A FEW YEARS AGO, I WAS FORTUNATE ENOUGH TO MEET Jorge Croda through a mutual friend. As Jorge and I got to know each other, it became clear that we had some personal and professional beliefs in common. Chief among them was the concept that golf offers wonderful opportunities and learning tools for growth in life that extend far beyond the sport. We have both felt compelled over the years to "give back" to others through the game of golf and that led us to cement a great friendship between us and the common goal of sharing the gift of golf with everyone.

My personal journey into golf began by accident when I was just eleven years old. I didn't realize it at the time, but the sport would become a catalyst for my journey into adulthood. At the time of this writing, I have now played golf for fifty years and I can honestly say that golf has shaped and shaped me both personally and professionally in a deep and meaningful way. Almost everything I am as a husband, father, teacher, coach, leader and friend has been influenced by golf and its many inherent values and learning opportunities. Golf has taken me to amazing places, helped me meet wonderful people and guided me to my current position as Executive Director of First Tee - Fort Worth. I am fortunate to be involved in the act of gifting thousands of young people in our community with this lifelong game that is associated with life skills and character development tools.

In Jorge I have found a kindred spirit. His journey through the game of life and golf has been different than mine, but has certainly been marked by the same learning, inspiration and opportunities. Jorge would be the first to tell you that he too has been indelibly changed for the better by his love of golf, and believes it can be a positive and uplifting life tool for building a successful existence. Based on the lessons learned in golf, Jorge has often overcome extreme circumstances and pressure situations to experience amazing success in his personal and professional pursuits. At the core of Jorge's belief system is the concept of servant leadership, which led him to explore and develop ways to help others succeed through key concepts in learning golf that also apply to life.

Now it is your turn to learn from Jorge and the contributors to this book about the power of golf to build a fulfilling life. I invite you to dive into this book and, hopefully, reading it will give you an idea of why golf is a metaphor for life and how it can provide you with fundamental learning opportunities, growth, physical and mental health and the power of friendship, as well as the ability to serve and lead others by playing a sport that can last a lifetime. From the opening pages, which dispel myths about golf, to the scientific and practical applications that will help you better understand the layers that make the game so engaging, Jorge will guide you down a path of curiosity and discovery.

If you're a long-time golf enthusiast, or have never picked up a golf club in your life, I think you'll be inspired to join the ranks of golfers who are continually learning through the sport.

Enjoy and hope to see you in the field!

Kevin Long
Executive Director First Tee - Fort Worth
Life Long Golfer and Learner

#GOLFLIFESTYLE

BOOST YOUR INGENUITY AND LEADERSHIP
SKILLS WITH THE FUNDAMENTALS OF GOLF AS A
LIFESTYLE.

Join the challenge of millions inspired by the fundamentals
of golf.

TABLE OF CONTENTS

INTRODUCTION

 "It is your decisions, not your conditions that determine your life."

— ANTHONY ROBBINS

With this book I sincerely hope that your innate curiosity will be awakened, that you will see and consider the fundamentals of golf as an instrument of development, evolution of your personal and professional life. And be careful! I am suggesting you grow and improve from learning the fundamentals of golf, not from the practice of golf itself... although my recommendation would be to integrate both so that you and those around you, in all areas of your life, can enjoy... yes... enjoy! The benefits that the practice of this sport so complete -although sometimes it is very misunderstood and misinterpreted- offers us.

You will see that the skills you acquire through golf come to the fore at the right and precise moment, whether you are at home, at a party or at work, you will be able to remain calm in difficult or complex situations, your confidence will become evident, you will surprise yourself by the ability you develop to control stress. At work you will be able to make decisions based on perfectly well oriented strategies, and your ability to concentrate and your capacity for teamwork and leadership will be amazing. You will see that these qualities, both in perseverance and honesty, are acquired, cultivated and developed naturally along the lines of golf and its fundamentals, because the practice of this sport strengthens both body and mind.

I venture to say this based on my years of experience in the golf world as a player, as an instructor, as a course superintendent and as an ambassador for the golf industry.

This book is a guide in which I share all the good things that golf has brought to my life, but, above all, it is a book with which I wish to thank this magnificent sport for all the benefits it has brought me and thanks to which today I can have the satisfaction of considering myself a good son, brother, student, collaborator, professional, husband, father, grandfather, good person, a better leader and a more responsible citizen, who enjoys with serenity and freedom the emotional and material success, husband, father, grandfather, good person, a better leader and a more responsible citizen, who enjoys with serenity and freedom the emotional and material success... and as the best way to thank is to share, here I leave you everything I have experienced, learned and lived so that you can make it yours and transform your days into a full life.

1

LIES, MYTHS AND BAD REPUTATION OF GOLF

> Golf is the closest game to the game we call
> life. You get bad luck from good shots; you get
> good opportunities from bad shots - but you
> have to play the ball as you find it.
>
> — BOBBY JONES

TO START PROPERLY, I THINK WHAT WE HAVE TO DO
first is to define golf as well as possible.

Golf is a sport that requires precision to introduce a ball,
with the least number of strokes possible, in the holes that
are distributed in the golf course. To do this, the golfer uses
clubs that differ slightly from each other, depending on the
type of stroke he/she needs to make. Each golfer can play
with a minimum of five clubs and a maximum of fourteen.
On the other hand, professional golf courses have 18 holes,
although there are also courses with 9 holes and to complete
the 18 holes of a standard round, two rounds are played.

This is a definition that objectively describes this sport, although it does not clarify or help to define the great benefits that its practice brings to the lives of golfers, professional or not; nor does it help to demolish the negative myths that have been created around golf... let's see some of them to see that it is not really necessary to continue believing in these myths, we will see that golf:

IS FOR THE ELITES: in reality it is not. In most countries there are public courses and very affordable and even free introductory courses; in fact, it is available to everyone without any distinction... in fact, some countries are integrating introductory golf programs for their public-school students.

And as this is not exactly a popular sport, what is not known is that many of the golf professionals come from families with few resources, but with a lot of desire to be someone in life and have managed to forge on the golf courses, so this is a sport that inspires you to grow.

IS EXPENSIVE: in reality, it is no more expensive than the average sport. We must remember that every sport or hobby involves an investment. Getting started in golf, or in any other sport or activity, requires an initial investment that may vary depending on many factors, but once this stage is over, golf is a sport even more economical than many others... in fact, it is suggested to start with a used equipment, you do not need to start in golf with a new equipment, so, once you have developed your *swing*, then you can go to a professional to help you choose the equipment that best suits your needs.

In addition, the list of physical, emotional and psychological benefits is so long that not only justifies the investment, but also goes hand in hand in this book, so I advise you to browse the internet and look for articles on the benefits of golf to our health.

IT IS NOT EASY TO LEARN: golf is not difficult, it is a sport that requires a lot of technique and therefore a lot of practice, however, when you start learning the basics in an easy, simple and fun way, it is very rewarding.

And believe me, once you learn the golf technique, it will serve you for life, since there is no age limit for this sport, and most importantly, the practice of this technique is not restricted to the limits of the golf courses, in fact, it will serve you to get ahead in life itself, you can put it into practice in your day to day.

IT'S NOT FUN: not at all! It will only take one round for you to realize that the time has flown by and that you have been able to completely escape from the problems and stresses of everyday life... you'll see that it even becomes addictive.

IT TAKES A LOT OF TIME: this statement is true if we count time in absolute hours as such... but if you have taken a moment to read the article recommended in the section "Golf is expensive", then, it is clear that for the countless and unimaginable benefits that golf brings us, all time is little time and it cannot be better spent... not to mention that you can play it alone, with company, during the day, at night and almost always... in countries with extreme climates, there may be times when it is better to simply enjoy the benefits that this sport brings to our private, social and work life.

FEW PEOPLE PLAY IT: the truth is that more and more people are interested in practicing this sport due to the great physical, psychological, emotional, social, work and business benefits it brings... yes! One of the qualities of this sport is integrity, and whoever plays it, is usually of integrity too... this is one of the reasons why it "seems" to be an uncommon sport... and in reality, it is not.

DAMAGES THE ENVIRONMENT: on the contrary! The trend is to build golf courses in abandoned areas, which means a landscape improvement in favor of the flora and fauna of the place where the course is located. The other trend for the maintenance of golf courses is to use recycled water for irrigation, and another great benefit to consider is that it helps to reduce soil erosion.

IT DOES NOT CONTRIBUTE TO THE ECONOMY: the truth is that golf generates and promotes investment in courses, hospitality, machinery, commercial and communication activities, real estate and tourism, and also creates direct and indirect jobs. On the other hand, it is a sport that does not receive subsidies, it is self-supporting, and all these false myths are an obstacle for golf to be seen as a popular sport that has the support and sponsorship of brands and companies.

BENEFITS SPECTATORS' HEALTH: The University of Edinburgh, in conjunction with the *Golf & Health Project*, published new research on the health benefits of golf spectators, showing that those who attend golf events may derive similar benefits to players. The study is the first to assess the physical activity of spectators while watching a golf match and shows that, of the fans surveyed, 82.9% met the recommended daily step count levels by achieving an average of 11,589 steps.

The truly regrettable aspect of this situation is that, by keeping these myths alive, golf is being prevented from reaching the vast majority of the population, who are being deprived of the personal, social and employment benefits that golf can bring them.

The healthiest way to bust and debunk these myths, in addition to refuting - as we have done above - each of them, is to detail only some of the main benefits of golf, since detailing them all would be a never-ending task:

It is also important to emphasize that the practice of golf provides a series of personal benefits that favor the preservation of the physical and mental integrity of the people, we can highlight the following:

- Walking between seven and ten kilometers improves cardiovascular health, regulates blood pressure, and keeps triglycerides and cholesterol at bay. If for some reason you cannot walk this distance, there is the alternative of doing it in a buggy, which contributes to mental health due to the placidity of the vehicle and the tranquility of the landscape.
- Tones the muscles of the arms, legs, back, thorax, abdominals and lumbar spine
- Improves coordination, balance and flexibility
- Oxygenates the blood and boosts vitamin D synthesis, so bones are strengthened and circulation improves.
- As it is not a high impact sport, it does not damage the joints like other sports, nor is it demanding in terms of physical strength, therefore there are no age limits to practice it.

- It improves mental health because the concentration and strategy that golf requires allows the player to disconnect from daily worries when focusing all his senses and efforts on his game... it makes you be present.

- It is an individual sport, but it allows players of different sexes, ages, levels... to participate in the same game, so it can be a family and friend's sport.

- Encourages new friendships and improves social relationships by providing the opportunity to interact with other people.

- It transmits values such as effort, perseverance, trust, courtesy, integrity, good judgment, honesty... all of which are highly valued in business and in life.

- Instills punctuality, which implies order, discipline, respect, responsibility, sense of fulfillment, good habits, self-demanding, planning, efficiency, effectiveness, and many other qualities that can be summarized in the phrase: "punctuality is the soul of courtesy".

- With each stroke you learn to control the ball, your body and your mind, which will develop levels of patience and serenity that you thought were unattainable.

- You will be aware of how your frustration tolerance is raised, because golf is like life, not everything is perfect.

- ...All this is done in contact with nature for hours... a perfect anti-stress effect. What more could you ask for?

SOCIAL AND LABOR BENEFITS.

It is important to recognize that the game of golf provides players with fundamental social skills, since it generates communication skills to learn to relate to people from different backgrounds from common references learned in the golf environment, i.e., golf carries its own language for the execution of the sport but this transcends to a language that allows a common dialogue between players and assistants which results in a harmonious social environment and positive relationship. Similarly, golf is presented as a medium in which the interactions that occur between different people with different skills and professions lend themselves to create, generate or propose work actions that originate as a product of trust and empathy that arises in the field of learning and practice of golf.

Specifically, the following social and labor benefits can be highlighted:

- Helps develop self-control because it teaches anger and rage management/elimination.
- Develops concentration as it is a basic and indispensable requirement for playing golf.
- Boosts self-esteem; as your game progresses you will feel more confident and secure.
- Provides an opportunity to develop and practice camaraderie with friends and playmates.
- Demonstrate your honesty by controlling the number of hits.
- Drives perseverance.
- Promotes competitiveness.

- You train your decision-making skills... every stroke is a decision.
- You learn the importance of listening to your intuition.
- You learn to interpret and understand character, personality and human behavior in playmates.
- Boosts confidence in personal, work and business relationships.
- Provides the opportunity to meet people from different professions with the consequent job, professional and business opportunities.

I can summarize all these qualities by describing my own experience with this sport throughout practically my entire life: "Golf taught me to know my limitations, to accept my frustrations, to respect others and not to lie even to myself".

GOLF AND CHILDREN.

So far, we have talked about the benefits of golf for adults... and what about children? These, as well as young people, turn out to be the most benefited population, since any sport that is learned from childhood gives the practicing child not only a healthy environment, but also a propitious space to grow in values of all kinds, as well as learning the importance of discipline for any dimension that is assumed in the course of life, in addition you can advance from learning for fun to professional golf practice and for this starting during childhood is the best decision.

This dimension is presented as a wonderful complement to school life and the construction of primary socialization, that is, more than learning content, which is important, golf helps to train the child for family and school interaction based on relationship codes to live together in society that will be useful for the rest of life, helping the child to think about guiding his life towards the best purposes and excellence.

As a second aspect, it is possible to reflect on **golf for children**, i.e., this sport has a whole foundation, training, support, training programs, counseling, practices, tournaments, among other aspects that are designed in the key of childhood, i.e., there is a whole theoretical, instructional and professional foundation that guarantees learning, practice and personal growth from childhood by the preparation in the sport of golf.

Finally, it is important to contemplate **golf with childhood**, since, as a product of the two previous considerations, golf from childhood and golf for childhood, it is evident the multiplicity of contributions that golf offers to children for the consolidation of the human person, that is, a being with personal and collective values that allows him/her to perform as an individual who contributes positively to society.

The ideal is to inculcate this sport in children from the age of six, which is the best age to start practicing this sport because:

- It is fun and "hooks" children quickly as they advance and improve faster than in other sports.
- Allows them to interact with adults and family members.
- It allows them to develop socialization and human relations skills.

- Promotes positive competition.
- Promotes fair play among participants.
- Empowers decision making.
- Encourages the desire to excel; child has fun breaking records.
- It teaches to value and respect nature by being in permanent contact with it during the game.
- The discipline inherent in this sport will naturally become part of the child's behavior.
- Helps to gain autonomy.
- Relaxes the body and mind, improves concentration.
- Improves and perfects fine and gross motor skills.
- Improves coordination, balance and equilibrium.
- Improves spatial location and laterality skills.
- Stimulates literacy and mathematical thinking.
- Develops critical and creative thinking skills.
- Promotes effort (frequency, timing, rhythm and emotion).
- Training in values such as Respect, Responsibility, Confidence, Courtesy, Honesty, Integrity, Perseverance, Punctuality, etc.

In summary, we can say that golf allows children to positively channel their emotions and enhance their qualities. These positive elements carry over into the rest of their lives and improve balance and overall performance.

Can you imagine being able to enjoy, from an early age, the benefits that golf offers for the development and potentiation of the innate qualities of the human being?

GOLF AND INCLUSION.

Now let's go one step further, let's talk about inclusion in golf, and let's talk about golf for people with disabilities or special needs. No, don't let that sound strange... on the contrary! Thanks to the inherent values of this sport, any golf course becomes the ideal environment in which people with any particular condition and who apparently cannot perform some functions, can actually do so, since it improves some of their physical and mental abilities, within an aura of respect and tolerance according to the characteristics of each case. It can be seen that golf in the key of inclusion has a bet where religion, economic status, sexual orientation, gender, ethnicity and in particular the physical or mental condition, are not excluding, on the contrary, "*everyone is welcome*".

It is important to clarify that this is a reality, timid yet, but it is giving convincing results and surely very soon many countries will join Argentina and Spain, which are the nations where we currently find golf courses with special programs for people with particular conditions. Based on the interview made in 2015 to Nora Lelczuk Goldfinger in the web channel Down21.org of the Ibero-American Foundation Down21, we can conclude that thanks to these programs, many people with disabilities manage to learn and enjoy this sport components, because they can:

Achieve the goals achieved by able-bodied players and set an example for society.

- Receive the same stimuli as any other player, in addition to participating in the same environments.

This helps them learn the guidelines for a natural coexistence in any environment.

- Improve in mathematics because they learn the concepts of direction, distance, force and space. In addition, by having to keep track of the number of strokes, they also improve their addition skills.
- Improve physically because the movements of golf serve as rehabilitation.
- Improve coordination.
- Improve mood.
- Stimulate and improve the relationship with parents, family and society in general.
- Learning to understand and follow rules in a fun way.
- Acquire, like any other athlete, values such as responsibility, companionship, solidarity, respect, organization, joy, among others.
- Making family and friends proud thanks to the happiness and joy with which they live their progress, but, above all, allowing a favorable feedback in all their environments.
- To be a testimony so that other people are encouraged to practice it.

So, if we keep an open mind to all the possibilities that we can look for and find, or that can be presented to us to get started in the world of golf, you will see that any effort is not only worth it, but it is little compared to all the benefits that this magnificent sport can give us to make our life become a healthy, balanced, profitable, coherent and happy existence.

I believe that at this point we can leave the myths aside... a golf ball, a club and a small space in your home are enough to start this adventure that will undoubtedly cease to be a hobby or a simple test and will become a lifestyle... a new life... your life!

> The image of golf is always linked to the fact that it is an elitist sport, expensive and for old people; nothing more out of reality, there are many examples of practice facilities and golf courses, that if we took a picture every morning, we could see that all customers are like you and me ... These myths of golf, do much damage to golf, away from popular sports because people simply have a wrong image already preconceived. Already when they see the word golf, they are prejudiced and think it is a sport inaccessible to them.
>
> — *TESTIMONY OF J.F. (HE STARTED GOLF IN HIS YOUTH)*

> I have firsthand experience of what the sport of golf through First Tee has achieved in my children after 10 years forming their character, strengthening values and life skills such as communication, self-control, goal setting, and overcoming challenges, in addition to living with diversity in inclusion, helped them to be good people and more responsible citizens.
>
> — *TESTIMONY OF R.C (A PARENT)*

" I have had the opportunity to learn the fundamentals of the game with minimal investment and using a reasonable amount of time. In my mind all the myths that exist about golf have been demolished, instead, I have found many benefits for my personal life, my family's life and my professional life. The values and skills learned from this sport are essential for life.

— *TESTIMONY OF A. S. (INITIATED IN GOLF AS AN ADULT)*

MENTAL CONCENTRATION EXERCISES:

#1 THE WALK OF AROMAS. Choose a park or a path that you particularly like and go for a walk. As you walk, pay attention to the different smells and aromas around you. Focus on a particular one that you like and bask in it. You will see how it intensifies as your concentration on that smell increases. Purpose: to enjoy the golf course, because it gives you inner peace.

#2 THE TWO-MINUTE TECHNIQUE. You will need a watch with a second hand. The game consists of focusing your attention solely and exclusively on the second hand, following its path around the watch face with your eyes. At first you may be caught thinking about other things. When this happens to you, start again and try to think and concentrate only on the hand of the watch. You should do

YOUR BEST SHOT

this twice, that is, for two minutes. Purpose: to achieve self-control in order to learn and play in inner peace, free of anxiety.

#3 THE GLASS OF WATER. Take a clear glass and fill it halfway with water. Then, take it with the hand of your choice and stretch your arm up to the height of your eyes. The goal is to hold the contents of the glass still for at least 3 minutes. Purpose: Mastery and control of the body to be attentive to the training process and to play with mastery and certainty.

ACTIVITIES DERIVED FROM THE CHAPTER:

- Choose one of the myths about golf and explain in your own words why it is not true:
- How you would encourage someone else to make the decision to take up golf?
- What do you consider to be one of the most important values that someone who plays golf learns? Explain your answer:
- What would you highlight about golf's relationship with children and people with disabilities?

2

LEARNING INTELLIGENCES AND NEUROSCIENCE

> If you think you can't get better, you don't know anything about life.
>
> — RAFAEL NADAL

THE PATH THAT LINKS THE WORLD OF EMOTIONS AND learning is intelligence, and this is developed in the most complex organ of the human body, the brain. Thanks to intelligence we can perform a myriad of functions and tasks such as reasoning, speaking, dreaming, feeling emotions, loving, laughing, crying, etc. As it is known, the information of everything that surrounds us reaches the brain through the senses, then, it processes all this information to give it sense and meaning.

The brain also biologically performs the function of controlling and being responsible for our digestion, breathing, blood circulation and body temperature.

Likewise, intelligence is not something fixed or determined, it is more like a multiplicity of windows that you can open or keep closed, but when you open them, you begin to discover things, you begin to understand, to associate, to create... and everything indicates that both intelligence and learning are closely related to curiosity, as stated by Francisco Mora: "Curiosity is the key that opens the windows of attention and with it learning and memory and with what has been learned and its classification, the acquisition of new knowledge".

Thanks to advances in science, it has been possible to carry out several studies that relate learning and curiosity, indeed, it seems that curiosity is what drives learning, preparing the brain to learn and memorize in the long term, but it goes even further, it turns out that curiosity also influences and is crucial for the development of talent, because talent is developed on something that catches our attention and interests us, this makes us delve into that which has conquered us to achieve excel in developing specific skills and abilities.

When something awakens our interest and curiosity, we tend to react positively, our emotions are effective, we are able to focus and fix our attention, making difficult decisions becomes less complicated, reaching incredible levels of perseverance in order to achieve our goals, because when we are interested in something out of curiosity, we are actually motivated and this motivation is what pushes us to do whatever is necessary, insisting and persisting, until we reach our goal.

It is for all these reasons that we must pay the utmost attention to curiosity, it is a driving force towards a productive and interesting life and, above all, we must encourage and promote it in our children and in ourselves.

Returning to intelligence, and although it is not known for sure in which part of the gray matter the intellect resides, nor what makes one person more intelligent than another, the truth is that intelligence lies in the brain, which is a muscle that, like any other muscle in our body, needs to be trained to achieve a higher and better performance. To train the brain you need perseverance, dedication and a healthy diet... remember throughout the book what we are saying in these lines... your brain has an immense capacity to improve and develop! Remember this because as you read this guide to the benefits of playing golf, you will see to what extent your brain, which is responsible for absolutely all our functions, can benefit.

In this sense, golf is a sport that, due to its characteristics of individuality, constancy, playing time, need for attention and concentration, is an excellent physical and mental training that involves the five senses and has enormous potential when it comes to learning more about how we think and act and that requires a permanent relationship with brain functions.

Thanks to scientific advances and neuroscience, today we know that there are nine different intelligences and that it is not as easy as before to define someone as intelligent or not intelligent, because if the concepts are explained to you based on the type of intelligence you have -which is how it should be- you will be able to understand them perfectly and effortlessly, otherwise, it is perfectly normal that you do not understand them.

These nine types of intelligence, according to Howard Garner, are:

#1 SPATIAL INTELLIGENCE: It is the intelligence that allows us to interact and understand the spatial and/or three-dimensional environment.

#2 LINGUISTIC INTELLIGENCE: That of our different languages, of words. It is not only limited to the verbal but also to the ability to communicate.

#3 LOGICAL-MATHEMATICAL INTELLIGENCE: The relationship between logic and mathematics maintains a direct and interdependent link with machines. We make them in our image and likeness and we adapt to them. It has to do with analytical and reasoning capacity.

#4 KINESTHETIC-SPATIAL INTELLIGENCE: It is the intelligence of our body, its movements and its gravitational conquests.

#5 MUSICAL INTELLIGENCE: Just as there is visual intelligence, musical intelligence has to do with the ability to express, transform, listen to and appreciate music, as well as to compose or perform it.

#6 INTERPERSONAL INTELLIGENCE: It is the intelligence of our internal processes to relate to others. It has to do with our ability to understand others and what is happening to another individual at a given moment or circumstance.

#7 INTRAPERSONAL INTELLIGENCE: This intelligence is not about the "other", but about oneself, the inward dialogue. It has to do with our ability to recognize who we are and what we really want, without deception or the interference of emotions.

#8 NATURALISTIC OR ENVIRONMENTAL INTELLIGENCE: The one that gives us attention to our natural environment. This type of intelligence is related to the ability to observe and reflect on what happens in our environment.

#9 EXISTENTIAL INTELLIGENCE: It has to do with the search for transcendence, for distant and not near ends.

Knowing that all these types of intelligence exist is really wonderful because, although we do not want to recognize it, when we are faced with a new project, an unusual situation, or a dilemma, we tend to doubt our intelligence and our capabilities; -how many times have we asked ourselves if we are capable... -and how many times have we answered: "I can't, I am not capable"! Because learning something new is to go out of our comfort zone, it is to take a step into uncertainty, it is to go beyond what we know and control, beyond what is predictable...

We experience fear, and that fear makes us feel, at the same time, that learning is based on coercion and obligation, when in reality learning should be a process based on need, on desire... on inspiration! ... Because if you believe it, you create it!

Before talking about education and the direct relationship it has with golf, I would like to comment and take into consideration the influence that fear has on learning:

It is completely and absolutely natural to feel fear when things get complicated or difficult for us, because it creates an atmosphere of uncertainty, we cannot know or guarantee a positive outcome, it leaves open the possibility that we cannot, that we will not reach our goals or objectives and, obviously, seeing things in this way has negative and detrimental consequences at an emotional and cognitive level. The Atlantic newspaper in the U.S. published an article warning parents that "Students inhibit their curiosity and reduce their love of learning because of their fear of failure".

Timothy Vickery, a researcher at Yale University's Department of Psychology, states that "The whole brain "cares" about success and failure, about winning and losing". The truth is that, if we don't fail, we don't learn; as Henry Ford, the successful American inventor and father of mass production, said: "Failure is just the opportunity to start again in a smarter way". However, by way of protection, the brain avoids any situation that - according to our brain - represents a threat and, consequently, inhibits our ability to take risks, even if it is a risk, we are not facing for the first time.

Developing, empowering and strengthening our confidence and self-esteem allows us to face and lose the fear of failure, it even helps us to value the opportunities that are lost, to understand that failure also brings benefits. To understand that mistakes are great teachers that should not be repeated, it is necessary to be aware of our skills, abilities and talents, this will help us not to give up, to keep moving forward, progressing and evolving, always aware that not trying is the worst way to fail.

I leave below two *links* in which you can appreciate in detail and clarity the great quantity and quality of benefits that golf brings, so that you can learn to face with total naturalness and throughout your life this feeling so present in our lives as fear, which well conducted and channeled, turns out to be an ally and not an enemy:

- https://issuu.com/thefirsttee/ docs/2017_parents__guide_book_final_for_
- https://firsttee.org/programs/parents-guide-first-tee/

And far beyond fear, in these same *links* you will discover that golf not only provides you with a series of values and tools to learn to be happy, it also creates a healthy foundation in all aspects of the person to cultivate in a healthy way the most important implicit feeling in human beings: love... love for oneself, family, friends and society in general.

Then, when a person, regardless of his age and level of training, resolves to learn something new because he needs it, he says to himself: "I'll get going" and does it, even if a little voice inside him tries to dissuade him out of fear... that's when he starts to change the whole anatomy and physiology of his own brain.

This is why the key to educational transformation lies in understanding that if a person, whether a child or an adult, does not learn, it is not because he or she is not intelligent, but because we are not talking about the way in which that person learns: "The brain learns with different styles; it would be important for the educator to consider that the student learns in a visual, auditory, linguistic and logical way, has the ability to learn in a reflective, impulsive, analytical, global, conceptual, perceptual, motor, emotional, intrapersonal and interpersonal way [1]" ... this last sentence, doesn't it seem to you a perfect summary of all the benefits that the practice of golf brings?... yes, golf contributes directly to stimulate the brain to open not only windows, but also doors and opens them wide.

Now that we know that our windows can become great doors, we can delve a little deeper into the exciting world of neuroscience and learning aimed at success beyond any initial circumstance... including age, because the executive functions of the brain, which are those that allow us to adapt psychologically and successfully to the environment, are functions that are learned or strengthened.

Enrique Guldberg, in his monograph *The Emotional Game: From survival to transcendence*, tells us:

> ...99% of education, and indirectly of sports training, is directed to the rational and physical part of the situation to be solved, and we have forgotten the most important thing, we have forgotten the forces that dominate most of our actions, which are EMOTIONS.

There are two emotions that we must keep in mind: fear and love. Surely you have heard before that the opposite of love is hate... the truth is that the opposite of love is fear. Fear paralyzes us, keeps us in a state of survival, where stress, physical, emotional and psychological wear and tear dominate us and do not allow us to find solutions or to propose and execute corrective measures when appropriate; on the other hand, love allows us to transcend, as well as to reach a state of full consciousness from which we can dream and make decisions that lead us to achieve our goals.

The executive functions of the brain, which we have mentioned before, are important because they are the set of skills and processes that will help us reach that state that allows us to reach transcendence, so here it would be good to say what they are and explain a little about each of them:

#1 Reasoning: It is the faculty that allows us to solve problems, draw conclusions and learn consciously, by establishing causal and logical connections with events.

#2 Planning: It is the process of making decisions in order to achieve a desired future, taking into consideration the current situation and the internal and external factors that could influence the achievement of the objectives.

#3 Goal setting: It is a skill that is related to motivation and allows us to decide how to invest our energy and where to direct our behavior.

#4 Decision making: It is the ability that enables us to discern which option to choose among all those that may be presented to us.

#5 Start and completion of tasks: Starting a task at a given time is an important cognitive process, as is the ability to decide when an action should be completed.

#6 Organization: It is the ability to unify and organize information efficiently, conveniently and profitably.

#7 Inhibition: It is the ability that allows us to govern our actions by controlling our behavior. It gives us the ability to restrain certain impulses, stop certain actions and prevent certain information from interfering with or altering our behavior.

#8 MONITORING: It is the ability to maintain attention on a task and regulate what and how we are doing what we are doing.

#9 VERBAL AND NON-VERBAL WORKING MEMORY: It is the ability to store information to be used in the future both verbally and nonverbally.

#10 ANTICIPATION: It is the ability to foresee in advance the results of an action and/or its consequences.

#11 FLEXIBILITY: It is the competence that allows us to change or adapt our way of acting or thinking in the face of probable changes in the environment. It also allows us to modify ongoing actions.

We have the case of Dr. Carlos E. Climent, who already in his eighth decade of life and thanks to the book *Golf and the Spirit* by the American psychiatrist M. Scott Peck, decided to venture into the world of golf. Regarding his experience with golf, Dr. Climent affirms that it is still a difficult learning process because it is a sport that has about 30 thousand variables... can you imagine the amount of new neuronal connections that this implies, the learning capacity has to be enhanced in an incredible way... and that after the age of eighty... imagine the wonders that can work in the brain of a child or adolescent!

On the other hand, and always according to Dr. Climent's experience, golf also boosts:

- Intuition, directly related to the decisions that must be made throughout life.

- Constant and tenacious training, which is how life should be faced and confronted.
- Tolerance to frustration, essential to not give up in the face of life's setbacks, but rather learn from them... to be resilient.
- The control of anger, fear, excessive optimism or pessimism, compulsive competition, self-recrimination, etc., because golf helps to exercise and keep the mind in silence and peace.
- Leadership through modesty, security and self-confidence; qualities totally opposed to exhibitionism.
- Humility, because the desire to win, is based on self-improvement and not on the fact of the opponent's defeat in the game.
- The qualities that prevent mistakes (flexibility, discipline, moderation, etc.) and not those that provoke them (stubbornness, ambition, anger, etc.).

Dr. Climent ends his article with the following quote: "An experienced golfer recently corrected me that, on all levels, but especially with respect to ethics, performance on the golf course is not that it has similarities with life: it is exactly like life! So, if you really want to get to know a person, invite them to play and you'll know where you stand." [2]

And now, if we move from golf for adults to golf for children, we will see the great qualities and values that this sport allows them to develop and that prepares them advantageously to achieve their goals throughout life, a life that will undoubtedly be profitable for themselves and for those around them due to the quality and quantity of qualities and benefits that golf brings them, such as:

- Promotes contact with nature.
- Combats sedentary lifestyles.
- Relaxes the body and mind.
- Improves flexibility, stability and motor coordination.
- Improves concentration and mental development as each stroke requires full attention and focus.
- Increases self-esteem because it is a sport in which progress is visible.
- Stimulates the desire to excel.
- Develops patience and increases tolerance to frustration.
- It favors decision making with each stroke because each stroke is a decision and the consequences must be assumed.
- Promotes fellowship.
- Contributes to emotional growth and development.
- It provides values such as fair play, sportsmanship, respect for rules and discipline.
- Democratizes team play as players of different levels and abilities can participate or compete on equal terms.
- Strengthens family ties.

So, if we have already said that golf is equal to life itself, now we can also say that it would also be a great school, because it is a sport that can be enjoyed with everyone, from family, friends and strangers ... that surely will become part of that group of great friends, in addition, golf teaches you to improve as a human being, respecting and honoring the game.

To say that golf would be a great school, you have to visualize with an open mind that all those who practice this sport also learn and share the values that golf teaches... and it's a very long list:

- We would be better people because life is seen and lived with simplicity.
- We would know how to greet and respect.
- We would be patient.
- We would know how to comply with rules, follow rules of courtesy and etiquette.
- We would be punctual and disciplined.
- We would know how to follow an order, keep still and be silent when necessary.
- We would be fair, correct and honest with everyone, including ourselves.
- We would know how to keep calm and temper.
- We would be respectful, committed, persevering and cooperative.
- We would know how to assume responsibilities and face any situation.
- We would be able to assume the consequences of our own decisions.
- We would know how to perform in an adverse environment and under pressure.
- We would be brave; we would not need to look for culprits for our inabilities or bad decisions.
- We would know how to live here and now, without being tormented by the past or terrified

by the future because the blows come one at a time.

All the above is powerfully connected with emotional management, as explained from neurosciences, that is, a person who learns not only the theory and practice of golf but in addition to these two elements acts with reflective intentionality, manages to connect the theoretical and practical intelligence, with the intelligence to self-manage emotions and behaviors, especially when these may be affecting negatively and transform them into positive actions for personal and social growth.

That is why, beyond the fact that golf is for everyone, it is a wonderful sport that helps to heal and mature the soul.

Yes, golf is a school that helps you live the best life possible... and yes, it is also true that we spend most of our lives working... so what does golf have to do with work?

 My father's story is that of a 69-year-old person, with hemiplegia, who decided to learn to play golf to strengthen his physical and mental health and to interact with several of his grandchildren who practice the sport. Today, with only one arm, he is able to shoot with wood, irons and, of course, putters. He also talks with his grandchildren about golf, so much so that Agustin, his 9-year-old grandson, designed for his grandfather on a piece of paper, a golf course with the names of the obstacles, some rules of the game and concepts such as: out of bounds, green, bunker, drop area, rough, fairway, approach, English terms, so that his grandfather does not forget them.

My father is moved to tears when he remembers that thanks to golf, he was able to share an activity with his grandchildren. My father states that he never imagined that he would be able to take out the club and share a day of play with his grandchildren.

— TESTIMONY OF A.D. (FAMILY MEMBER OF A HANDICAPPED GOLF PLAYER)

The role of the instructor is central because he/she must try to motivate students to discover principles on their own. Therefore, instructor and student must connect in an active dialogue for discovery.

In discovery learning, the teacher organizes the class so that students learn through active participation. In guided discovery, students are presented with intriguing questions, ambiguous situations, or interesting problems. Instead of explaining how to solve the problem, the teacher provides appropriate materials, encourages students to make observations, develop hypotheses, and test the results.

— TESTIMONIAL FROM P.R. (GOLF INSTRUCTOR)

" However, Jorge has taught us that each one of us is unique and unrepeatable and that we learn in different ways; he also showed us that the brain is a muscle that can be trained and that practice makes perfect, the fundamental role of emotions and that we ourselves put the obstacles in our way.

The obstacles we encounter on the golf course are found in life itself.

— TESTIMONY OF J. P.
(BUSINESSWOMAN WHO LEARNED
GOLF AS AN ADULT)

MENTAL CONCENTRATION EXERCISES:

#1 EXERCISES FOR ATTENTION. A sequence of numbers is communicated orally and the person has to remember them in the same order and in reverse order. The length of the sequence will increase progressively. (Purpose. To strengthen concentration in order to learn to assimilate important information).

#2 EXERCISES FOR PERCEPTION. A model image is presented together with others that represent the same object, but vary minimally in size. The person must perceive the one that corresponds exactly with the model. (Purpose: to learn to recognize and differentiate golf accessories).

#3 EXERCISES FOR COMPREHENSION. The subject is given a series of orders to execute. It is checked if the action corresponds to the order issued (Purpose: To learn norms, rules and behaviors for learning and execution of golf).

———

ACTIVITIES DERIVED FROM THE CHAPTER:

1. Which intelligence (is) do you identify with and why?
2. Choose an image (photograph) that explains one of the qualities or benefits of golf. (If you are in a group, share it and explain it to a partner).
3. Elaborate an alphabet soup with 15 values that the practice of golf gives you.

GOLF AND WORK

> The road to success is always under construction.

— ARNOLD PALMER

IN THE PREVIOUS CHAPTER WE HAVE ALREADY DETAILED the great physical, emotional and psychological benefits that golf brings to those who practice this sport and all, absolutely all these benefits will result in the most important activity that occupies most of our time as human beings... our daily work! And when I talk about work, I am not only referring to the activity we perform at a professional level to generate an economic income that allows us to cover our basic needs and achieve our goals of self-realization, I am also referring to household chores and activities that we can perform in our society as part of it.

However, if we focus on the classic concept of work as that activity, we perform in order to develop our skills and obtain

JORGE J CRODA

an economic benefit in return, we have to recognize that the traditional work we all know is changing drastically, mainly as a consequence of the rapid and changing technological progress of recent years.

Indeed, in the near future, many of the jobs we know today will have disappeared due to the incursion of artificial intelligence, the internet of things or *big data*.

The new leaders will have a great capacity, above all, to adapt to change, but they will also be people with empathy, intuition, innovation, creativity and reasoning, all of which are qualities that are encouraged, fostered and developed. It is here where we can count on *coaching* for the great possibility it has to play important roles in achieving all these objectives in the key of powerful questions for positive decision making.

According to the report "The Future of Jobs 2018", published by the World Economic Forum, from the current technological advances, more than half of the current workforce will need to improve their skills in order to access new quality jobs, because not only technological skills will be needed, but also a whole series of competencies and soft skills, tremendously necessary to be exponential leaders and, again, we have here *coaching* as the great driver for the promotion of these skills, since it accompanies people towards the recognition and conquest of their potentialities from the understanding of the changes in the ecosystem and in oneself.

The new workers and professionals can be in any hierarchical position as they are characterized by being flexible and innovative, necessary and appropriate conditions that will be in high demand to work in the new times where special skills will be needed for the adoption of new technologies, the optimization of performance and expected results, as well as a great ability to adapt to changes... these will be the leaders of this new environment called VUCA[1] (volatile, uncertain, complex and ambiguous), who will also need to have the ability to co-create in a virtual environment with dispersed multicultural teams.

These profiles require some very well-defined skills:

- Ability to adapt to different contexts and environments.
- Creative, inventive and innovative ability to produce ideas.
- Ability to collaborate and motivate.
- Digital literacy and understanding of how and why digital technologies work.
- Learning capacity.
- Ability to solve unfamiliar problems in different contexts.
- Awareness of the value of open access to information.
- Continuous capacity for experimentation and formal and informal learning.
- Ability to use tools to solve different problems
- Competence to create horizontal knowledge networks.
- Absence of fear of failure

In reality, people born before 1981 are the ones who will have to make a special effort to adapt and internalize this new environment, background and way of working, as it seems that those born after 1980 -the millennials- have all or most of these qualities inherent in them.

In our society, where competition and competitiveness are really "wild", and where, as already mentioned, new technologies are rapidly and drastically changing the market, the need and capacity for creativity, intuition, flexibility, adaptability, patience, tolerance, etc., are absolutely necessary qualities to be able to stay in the market and achieve our objectives, which can be totally diverse and all valid.

All the aforementioned qualities, in addition to others such as self-esteem, the ability to concentrate and create strategies, control of emotions, perseverance, discipline, among others, are qualities that are developed and strengthened through the practice of golf.

Well, I think it's pretty clear how these qualities will positively affect our daily life at home, at work and in society, right? Because if we add up all the benefits that golf brings us, we can deduce that resilience and all that it brings us summarizes the practice of golf as a sport that benefits absolutely all aspects of our lives and our daily lives ... but what if we want to go a little further? If our desire is to become leaders in our companies and our lives, where the ability to negotiate is basic and essential to achieve our goals... can golf help us?

I think the best way to respond is to tell you about my own experience:

The beauty of a round of golf with clients and prospects is that it is five hours of soft selling who you are, your company, what you know and who you are. Each golfer spends only a few minutes hitting the ball, the remaining time is spent talking and getting to know our backgrounds, personalities and characters in a relaxed atmosphere, in a natural environment that invites naturalness and sincerity. It is also a propitious moment to initiate or motivate a coaching session.

Likewise, in a two-person game (twosome), not only can you make a wonderful business deal while the game is in progress, but you can also have a powerful coaching session and as part of my own experience, I have been able to use elements of coaching to motivate people to take up golf or improve their game.

On the golf course you know who is who, that is, the person in all its positive and negative dimensions and it is there where you show if you can be trusted or not, if you will get the job, the business or the promotion. This highlights another important aspect of golf's relationship with the business world.

Golf also provides better opportunities to build and deepen business relationships; a good golfer practices in life what he practices on the course: he gets excited when his client makes a good shot and his game is perfect, he doesn't get angry or lose control when his is not the best, let alone the expected one.

And here is a golden rule... I want to repeat that a good golfer practices in life what he practices on the golf course... **golf never lies, as you live you play and as you play you live...** that is why you can place your trust in those who are *fair players*, and as this rule also applies to you, it turns out that the business relationships established on golf courses are usually successful, long lasting and very satisfactory on a commercial and personal level.

When I talk to sales teams about playing business golf, I emphasize the importance of playing with proper etiquette and following the rules of golf; during the five hours that the game lasts, they have the opportunity to demonstrate their human and professional qualities that will undoubtedly lead to a solid business relationship... or, they will demonstrate that they are there only with the intention of getting some business without much interest or respect... believe me! It does not work! it doesn't work, the only thing you will achieve is to sabotage your business relationships instead of solidifying them and you may even be considered a toxic player... here, my sincere advice is to study, learn and be guided by the fundamentals of golf so you can become a successful human being, be happy in life and freely enjoy the benefits that golf will bring you, feeling worthy of them.

I want to end this chapter by making a short summary with the intention of clarifying and validating that golf is a great tool to motivate work teams because, although it is a sport that is basically practiced individually, it has some characteristics that make it the appropriate sport to strengthen the bonds between the members of a work team:

- Golf helps to create leaders and to reinforce the figure and image of the person who has the ability to guide colleagues, since the practice of this sport helps to promote initiatives, make decisions and design strategies.
- In golf, absolutely all participants play an important

role; this also applies to the caddie, who is the person in charge of carrying the clubs and without whose participation, the game and the result would not be the same. This philosophy, applied to work teams, makes us see that each of the members plays a fundamental and important role in order to achieve the defined objectives.

This playing philosophy allows players of all levels to participate in a game, allowing and encouraging everyone to feel valued and enjoy the game equally.

These characteristics of golf make it possible to strengthen the bonds between the members of a work team, establishes and maintains team spirit. Each golf game has a goal and everyone will participate to achieve it.

Now that we have seen that golf is an inclusive sport, which shows that individual play is only part of teamwork, where each of the participants has a unique and indispensable role, in the following chapters we will develop the individual capabilities, at the professional level, that golf provides and thanks to which you can easily and safely place yourself in the position you like the most and serve as a basis for developing your skills and gifts in your life.

> The golfer could explain the behavior of the company manager. "If you want to know a man's character, play golf with him." Today no one wants to play golf with this manager. According to testimonials from 'caddies' and fellow golfers, this manager is a sore loser, a liar, presumptuous and very cheating. In

addition, he does not recognize a defeat and is not kind to opponents who beat him.

It is undoubtedly a sport he is passionate about, as he does not need teamwork, he is the administrator of the place where he plays and the final score depends on his conscience.

His caddies always have golf balls in their pockets to place his boss's ball in better places, he lifts the ball four feet from the hole to avoid missing the shot, he lies about his handicap (supposedly 3.6) and does not allow trees or lakes to get in the way of his game; if his ball lands there, he will consider it unfair and play again. A little golf cheating or improper use of the rules for personal gain.

— TESTIMONIAL A R (BUSINESS OWNER)

The practice of golf also has an important component of socialization: it is a sport where one competes more against oneself than against other rivals, which promotes conversation for several hours. In fact, many deals are often closed on the greens, where each party observes the honorability, honesty and patience in the game.

— TESTIMONIAL FROM D.V. (CEO GOLF PLAYER)

Learning the fundamentals of golf allowed me to discover my strengths and weaknesses, while working on them. I was able to see my work from a different perspective, becoming a better collaborator. I learned to share with my colleagues, to take charge of myself, it led me to develop loyalty to the environment. It taught me to use my imagination and create the life I want, because what you create, you create.

Every stroke is a decision and golf is full of them, which we also apply to our work based on strategies.

— TESTIMONY OF R. T. (COMPANY SUPERVISOR, GOLF PLAYER)

MENTAL CONCENTRATION EXERCISES:

#1 EXERCISES FOR PROCESSING SPEED. The person is instructed to point out as quickly as possible and making as few mistakes as possible which of the symbols are equal to the model previously presented. (Purpose: to learn to choose the best move for each shot)

#2 EXERCISES FOR ORIENTATION. The person is placed in an unknown place and is given a map of the place. He/she must follow a route guided only by the map (Purpose: to know the golf course and the opponents before starting the game).

#3 EXERCISES FOR THE CALCULATION. The person must subtract 7 by 7 from the number 300. The person must do it mentally and trying to make as few mistakes as possible in the shortest time possible. (Purpose: to strengthen concentration during the game).

ACTIVITIES DERIVED FROM THE CHAPTER:

1. Analyze why the best time to initiate the assertive dialogue or effective negotiation or management required during a game of golf is on the fourth or fifth hole. (key words: Sensitizing, managing, timing -Timing)
2. Analyze the expression "golf never lies, as you live you play and as you play you live", particularly related to the business world.
3. Are you prepared for the VUCA environment? Yes? No? Why?

4

LEADERSHIP THROUGH GOLF

 Practicing and perfecting the art of leadership presents great similarities to the challenge of perfecting our game on the golf course.

— RAFAEL MARATEA

BEFORE TALKING ABOUT LEADERS, WE MUST BE CLEAR about what leadership is, we will define it as the skills to lead and manage that a person has, thanks to which he/she can influence the way of being or how a person or a work team acts, achieving that in an effective and proactive way the goals and objectives are reached.

In an effective team led by a leader there is no scale of power, rather, all members contribute in different ways to the success of the team, although, generally, the leader will have the ultimate responsibility because he/she possesses certain qualities such as attitudes, skills and abilities that allow him/her to take the initiative, delegate, promote, manage and motivate to bring any project to a successful conclusion in an efficient and effective manner.

It should be noted that a leader never imposes his ideas, since one of his obvious qualities is teamwork, and he ultimately determines the best of what is built as a group.

As we have seen in the previous chapter, the characteristics of the new workforce are changing and in the same way, new forms of leadership are needed that go hand in hand with the qualities of the workers according to the new norms, environments and trends, this is how neuroleadership is born; those who exercise this type of leadership are leaders who learn from psychology and neuroscience, practice resilience and the development of emotional control, aspects and qualities that can also be acquired, developed and enhanced with the constant practice of golf.

We are currently living in times of total anxiety and uncertainty. 2020, the year in which I am writing this book, is a year that clearly demonstrates that we are living in a world lacking leaders in absolutely every area we can imagine... this is the perfect year to be able to propose and assume changes... sometimes we have no alternative, but other times, it can be the alternative... and for that we need to develop our leadership skills and apply them to the area that calls us, seeks us and pleases us... we can lead our lives, our group, our community and beyond as far as we wish and feel comfortable.

Because, believe it or not, just by leading your life, you are already contributing to changing society and the world... shall we learn how? Let's see!

Rafael Maratea recently wrote his book *Liderar con Swing. Discover the art of leading through golf*, a publication that proposes an analogy between the capacities, aptitudes and conditions of a leader and golf, a solitary game but one that encompasses many conditions necessary to carry out good leadership, such as commitment, confidence, concentration, focus, abstraction, passion, anxiety, frustration, objective, strength, solitude, balance and also talent, among many other qualities. [1]

In the same book, Maratea also tells us:

> Playing is not a waste of time. On the contrary, one understands better how things work by observing concerns, doubts, fears and those needs and desires that cannot be expressed in words, but can be expressed through play and sport. In fact, one can see on a golf course many of those hidden or unknown attitudes that are rooted in our being...

And he continues:

> It is a game of sensations that teaches about strategy, concentration, visualization and positioning of objectives. It is useful for a leader to play golf because all the concepts that are needed on the golf course can be perfectly transferred to leadership.

Indeed, I have seen for myself that golf is a great teacher of leadership because it is:

. . .

#1 TEACHES HUMILITY.

Players need and seek the support of experts to improve their quality of play; they know that they can always improve and the only way to achieve this is to continue learning and practicing, putting humility before arrogance, calmly assuming the corrections or suggestions made to us. Accepting that no matter how much we advance in technique and practice we are always susceptible to improve.

#2 TEACHES LEADERSHIP.

A golf player and a leader never stop learning while maintaining the rhythm, a basic element to generate action in the game and in leadership, also within a favorable environment based on communication, healthy coexistence and objectives. Just as in golf, rhythm is a fundamental part of the game, in leadership, rhythm is the vital key to generate action, create a space of healthy coexistence and achieve challenging objectives in an atmosphere of camaraderie, communication and understanding of the teams. Both in golf and in leadership, the day to day is considered as wonderful moments to learn, grow, know and apply.

#3 COMPETITIVE.

It is a very favorable field to rub elbows with clients, connect with colleagues or make favorable links. Working relationships are consolidated in the field. It is in the game where decisions are made that allow linking with bosses and leaders of other companies. Practice benefits social skills needed to relate and communicate appropriately and assertively with others. Both promote fair play and recognition of others, understood as healthy competition and respect for oneself and others.

#4 EXCITING.

It favors affective, effective and business relationships between people. It is the balance in the life of the leader and his collaborators, it achieves that each one commits to perform the task, knowing that this will have repercussions in his particular life. The leader must find balance in his emotions and actions.

#5 RELAXES AND DE-STRESSES.

It provides the opportunity to enjoy an outdoor activity, to be in contact with nature, with all the benefits that this entails. It also favors the generation of endorphins that provides a sense of well-being and improves concentration. At the same time, an authentic leader is a being characterized by security and tranquility.

#6 PROMOTES COMMITMENT AND TRUST.

The player is committed to his game and knows that it is up to him to improve and achieve excellence. All golfers face their fears, it is part of the game. The more you play and the more you practice, the less fear you have because your confidence grows. Just as great golfers gain confidence through their training, the leader grows in confidence through his actions and decisions.

Tim Gallwey, who many consider the father of modern *coaching*, is the author of a series of books in which he establishes a new method for training and developing personal and professional excellence in a variety of fields that he calls *The Inner Game*. According to his theory, sports *coaching* is today the best tool for the development of our inner game because it helps us to know, recognize, accept and change our habits, to become aware of our limiting beliefs and thoughts, to know and recognize our emotions and feelings that affect us so much and to manage them to our benefit. *Coaching* helps us to prevent our concentration levels from dropping between holes, because that is when our deepest internal dialogues take place. With *coaching* we learn that by developing our **BEING** we improve our **DOING**, obtaining clearly different results.

Thanks to approaches such as those of Tim Gallwey and the values that are reaffirmed or acquired through golf, the central theme of this book, today we have people who have developed their leadership qualities to become coach-leaders. Coach-leaders are people who go a step beyond leadership as such and incorporate *coaching* tools, thanks to which they make it possible for different things to happen and improve the functioning of their team... in addition, we can affirm that the coach-leader comes down from the pedestal of the hierarchy to be at the service of his team, giving rise to what is called servant leadership.

A leader-coach will always be a helpful leader, a person who has developed qualities that allow him to be always attentive and available to those who are eager to improve all their skills and abilities in search of their evolution and happiness... and in fact, aren't we all on that path? Well, yes... at some point, we all need a *coach*.

And just as today we can find a helpful leader, we can also find that helpful *coach* who guides and accompanies you from the confidence that is born in love... and no! They are not words, because only thanks to that commitment will motivate and guide you towards a meaningful purpose and make your actions align with your goals, until your footprints precede the path of others.

As you can see, golf leads you to develop all the qualities you need to become a leader... and leading yourself is perhaps the first and hardest step to become a leader of social or business groups... so let's move on to our next chapter: self-leadership.

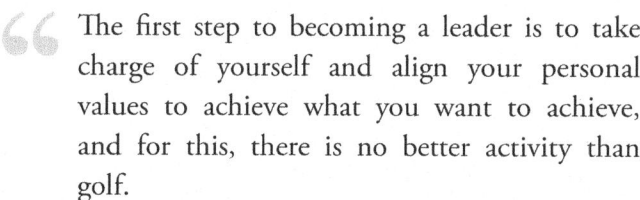

The first step to becoming a leader is to take charge of yourself and align your personal values to achieve what you want to achieve, and for this, there is no better activity than golf.

Both the golfer and the leader focus all their attention and efforts to serve the goal. Golf helps the leader to strengthen his leadership skills. On the golf course we are constantly making decisions, managing emotions and situations (adverse and favorable), we have to be agile and creative to avoid getting into obstacles or once inside them leave as little affected as possible in the pursuit of the goal.

— TESTIMONIAL FROM G.H.
(MANAGER AND GOLFER)

We learned that leadership springs from within, is built in the depths of the soul and emerges precisely in the service to others. It implies the ability to listen, because we do not know everything. It implies the ability to learn from others and therefore the ability to add the strengths and cushion the weaknesses of all to build a great team.

We have discovered that the power to change realities does not lie in our complaints, but begins within us, with our environments.

— TESTIMONY OF J.A.
(BUSINESSWOMAN GOLF PLAYER)

The contribution I see golf as making to leadership is as important as it is necessary. Through internalizing the fundamentals, you can tap into your talents and become the leader your people expect you to be. We know that not everyone can be a leader, however, the fundamentals give you the learning to understand leadership and allow you to lead others.

We also see the need to have a coach to accompany us on our journey as it will serve as a mirror where we can bounce our ideas.

— TESTIMONY OF S. G. (FATHER OF A FAMILY WHOSE SON PLAYS GOLF)

MENTAL CONCENTRATION EXERCISES:

#1 EXERCISES FOR EXECUTIVE CONTROL. The person is provided with a sequence of actions either visually through bullet points or verbally through written instructions. The person must read them carefully and order them creating an appropriate sequence of actions. (Purpose: to learn to delegate roles and functions in groups).

#2 EXERCISES FOR REASONING. A group of words is presented and the person must point out which is the one that is not related to the others. (Purpose: to learn how to generate work teams).

#3 EXERCISES FOR LANGUAGE. A word composed of certain letters is provided. The person will have to generate new words by combining the letters of the initial word (Purpose: to learn to propose alternatives when difficulties arise in the work group).

ACTIVITIES DERIVED FROM THE CHAPTER:

- Choose the name of a golfer that you consider has leadership qualities. Briefly explain your answer.
- Expand on one of the six relationships between golf and leadership with an example that can be applied to the practice of golf.
- Why does a leader-coach contribute to the construction of personal excellence?

5

SELF-LEADERSHIP

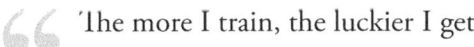 The more I train, the luckier I get.

— GARY PLAYER

To start with a simple and clear definition, let's say that self-leadership is being able to go through life following the line that is important to me and gives me the values I need to be happy and make my environment happy by being an example to follow, I can only be an example to follow if I am a coherent and congruent model... when I **AM** what I project... knowing that I learn from every teaching I give. It is about the permanent relationship that exists between being and doing.

It is also the ability to discern with clarity and precision what I want in my life and how I want my life... it is knowing how to locate my environments of triumph... only then will I be able to make my decisions and trace my life line according to my planned objectives in my family, social and work environment, among others; I will be able to face the consequences and become someone with total personal empowerment and control over my life. That is, when autonomy is put in function of permanently configuring the best version of myself, as a being in constant construction.

A person with self-leadership possesses a series of psychological and emotional skills that accompany him to achieve his goals, regardless of the resources he has or the uncertainty that surrounds him in the present or in the future; he is focused, persistent, disciplined, self-motivated, organized and with a great emotional intelligence based on optimism and resilience.

These last two qualities that we have mentioned, optimism and resilience, are determining factors in the attitude of a leader who has started from self-leadership.

In his book *Optimism and Health: What Science Knows about the Benefits of Positive Thinking*, Dr. Luis Rojas Marcos points out that optimism is the vaccine against hopelessness, and Susan C. Vaughan, in her book *The Psychology of Optimism: The Glass Half Full or Half Empty*, says: "Optimism is like a self-fulfilling prophecy. Optimistic people predict that they will achieve what they desire, they persevere, and people respond well to their enthusiasm. This attitude gives them an advantage in health, love, work and play, which in turn validates their optimistic prediction" ... unlike those who are not optimistic and who think they will fail and who do not give up until they do fail.

Resilience can be defined as the capacity of human beings to flexibly assume extreme situations, overcome them and emerge stronger, and the truth is that this capacity -which enhances happiness- can be possessed by a person, a community, an organization or a natural system. Resilience allows us to prepare ourselves for disruptions, to recover from shocks and stress, to adapt and grow from conflictive circumstances, and to learn with serenity from these tragic situations and emerge stronger from them.

Returning to our topic on self-leadership, we must detail that it meets five characteristics known as the **5 "S's" of** self-leadership:

#1 SELF-KNOWLEDGE. It is the ability to recognize and identify the way in which emotions and thoughts affect us and the origin of why they affect us; to do this we must be aware of our resources and strengths, as well as our limitations and weaknesses.

#2 SELF-ESTEEM. It is how a person sees and perceives him/herself; it is how he/she values and evaluates him/herself in terms of his/her own being, his/her way of existing and his/her qualities, accepting him/herself with respect and kindness, which allows him/her to empower him/herself as a person.

#3 SELF-AUTONOMY. It is the ability to establish priorities and objectives for oneself and independently, to make decisions, to assume the consequences of our own actions and to form personal criteria.

#4 SELF-MANAGEMENT. It is the ability to regulate our emotions, to have emotional self-leadership and to know how to direct our behaviors and resources towards a proposed goal, having the ability to analyze and direct our actions without help and redirect them if necessary.

#5 SELF-MOTIVATION. It is having the ability to influence and persevere in maintaining our own state of mind to achieve a set goal. This requires initiative, will, commitment, optimism and orientation towards the achievement of objectives.

It is also important to highlight that there are some characteristics and qualities that are needed for the achievement of a person with self-leadership skills:

- **You must know yourself:** analyze your qualities, your strengths and weaknesses so that you have an idea of what are your resources and what are your limitations. The resources to empower them and the limitations to overcome them.
- **Learn for yourself:** when you have identified your weaknesses and limitations, you should strive to obtain information to know these points very well so that you can find ways and means to improve them; it is also important to work on reinforcing your qualities and strengths.
- **The wheel of life:** this technique helps to analyze the present and focus on the future; you must draw a circle and write ten areas that you wish to change or improve, and you must number them assigning them a priority, obviously, with the intention of working on them.
- **Set objectives:** Now that you have identified your areas of work, you can set objectives that you can achieve and measure, but, above all, they must be

specific and concrete - if necessary, you can subdivide them - and you must assign them a short, medium or long term in your action plan to achieve your objectives.

- **Plan a strategy:** Remember that to achieve your objectives you must be consistent with the resources you have and the qualities that go with them; you must be very sensible about your faults and virtues.

- **Program:** do not be afraid to use the many tools that technology offers today to make programs and define plans, always taking into account the resources of time, personnel and materials; only in this way will you be able to make a realistic approach.

- **Focus:** to avoid any distractions, it is best to focus on one activity at a time.

- **Manage changes:** Every plan or program must include a plan B to face any problem or circumstance that may arise, but, if a setback is not controllable, it will be necessary to change the perspective and maintain the attitude, accepting this new situation as an opportunity.

- **Develop routines:** they will help you organize and order your days; discipline, perseverance and commitment are essential.

- **Self-motivate yourself:** it is necessary that you do not lose the habit of rewarding yourself for your achievements, which will also help you to maintain your good behavior and in this way, you will achieve a balance between the discipline of your developed routines and the gratification.

- **Allow yourself to be flexible:** you must know when

to stop so that your performance does not decline. You must be kind to yourself, you cannot and should not repress your emotions, and you must be consistent with your intellectual and work capabilities and your human qualities.

- **Make adjustments:** when necessary, remember that your plans and programs include flexibility to make changes when required based on evaluation and monitoring that is done from time to time to check that you are on track to achieve your objectives.
- **Make a final assessment:** analyze the entire path that has led you to your goal and internalize everything you can learn for the future.
- **Seek a professional:** remember that you can always turn to a professional to follow a training program towards self-leadership in general or just in some component that you feel you need to learn or reinforce.

So... what about golf? What does golf have to do with self-leadership...? Let's see!

Well, the truth is very simple, it turns out that we are in life as we are on the golf course. This means that since golf is one of the most complete, coherent and challenging sports, it allows us to see life in a concrete, precise, real and practical way. Thanks to golf we can know how we are and based on this knowledge and the fundamentals of golf, we can improve, rectify and change from the physical, mental and emotional points of view.

In golf and in life we can find some common ground:

- **Tenacity:** only with tenacious, constant and persevering practice can perfection be achieved... both in golf and in leadership.
- **Security:** it is absurd to deny that one always feels fear before something new, a new shot or a new project. Only practice and constant improvement will replace this fear with confidence and security. The mettle needed to achieve a perfect shot is based on many of the qualities that a good leader needs... let's not forget that!
- **Concentration:** is the ability to abstract from everything that surrounds and can mean an unnecessary and even fatal distraction, so that, both in golf and in leadership, it is necessary to focus and think only and exclusively about what needs to be done.
- **Balance:** it is necessary to have harmony between the body and the mind, the physical and the emotion; let's not forget that a clear mind is decisive. "A healthy mind in a healthy body".

We can say then, that golf is a sport not only of strategies, concentration, visualization and positioning but also of sensations because basically, this sport undresses you... it reveals what you really are, and if you have understood, learned and internalized the values and fundamentals of golf, you will translate them into any project you have to lead, you will be able to make the right decisions, you will make the right choices, you will be aware of your resources, you will know how to maintain and instill calm... you will be able to teach without ever stop learning.

We must remember, feel and know that golf is an honest game that reveals you to yourself and others and polishes your essence, polishes your **BEING.**

> Within learning the fundamentals of golf self-leadership has helped me to be proactive, disciplined and an independent decision maker. People who do not have a strong sense of this quality tend to feel they are not in control of themselves, often lack focus and are easily overwhelmed.
>
> By offering a long-term perspective on your life - both personally and professionally - self-leadership will give you a broader, holistic mindset.
>
> — TESTIMONY OF B.R. (UNIVERSITY STUDENT WHO LEARNED GOLF IN HIS YOUTH)

> Today I am a person more aware of who I am, which allows me to identify what I can do, what I can give when working in a team and in my personal relationships. I learned to face challenges in a different way through action and solution. On the other hand, I am a person who learned to work effectively in a team, to build interpersonal relationships through trust. Building confidence in myself and in what I am and can become.

— TESTIMONIAL FROM F.C. (YOUNG
PROFESSIONAL LEARNING GOLF).

 Having learned the fundamentals of golf, its
values, attitudes and skills is a tool that gives us
the ability to intentionally and consciously
influence our own thoughts, emotions and
behaviors in order to achieve personal goals; it
also allows us to recognize the importance of
self-knowledge, self-esteem, autonomy, self-
management and self-motivation, which leads
us to discover our talents and super-powers
through which we design the life we want and
develop the ability to remain calm in difficult
situations.

In short, for golf to flow properly, you must
have harmony in that unity of body, mind,
spirit and environment that teaches us to be
present and focused.

— TESTIMONIAL BY P. F.
(PROFESSIONAL WHO LEARNED
GOLF AS AN ADULT)

MENTAL CONCENTRATION EXERCISES:

#1 REVIEW YOUR DAY: to end the day it would be ideal to do
another meditation before going to sleep. After this, when

you lie down in bed, do a review of what you have done during the day. Do not dwell on judgments, just try to review the different things you have done, as if you wanted to write them down in a list, nothing more. With a little perseverance in practicing these exercises, you will see that your ability to concentrate improves day by day. (Purpose: to self-evaluate one's daily life with a view and goal to become the best version of oneself).

#2 PHOTOGRAPH WITH YOUR MIND: look around you and choose an object, no matter what it is. Observe it carefully. Think about it, what it is for, what it is made of, what color or texture it has. Then make a kind of mental photograph of it. Now, close your eyes and recreate in your mind that object in detail. (Purpose: to learn to visualize valuable moments of training and practice in order to become better and better each day).

#3 MAKE FRIENDS WITH MATHEMATICS: calculation is one of the activities that strengthen concentration the most, since a high level of concentration is essential to perform mental operations. Try to practice activities such as sudokus or any mathematical operation on a regular basis. You will see how after a while you will notice a great improvement in your ability to concentrate. (Purpose: to strengthen the memory to learn and recognize our qualities, not forget them).

ACTIVITIES DERIVED FROM THE CHAPTER:

1. Write a short story, tale, poem or anecdote where you incorporate the **5 "S's"**.
2. Elaborate the graph of the wheel of life.
3. Analyze a concept in which golf and self-leadership are related.

6

LEADING ENVIRONMENTS OF SUCCESS

 What do you hang on the walls of your mind?

— EVE ARNOLD

WHEN WE TALK ABOUT ENVIRONMENTS OF TRIUMPH, TRY asking someone: in what environments do you move, you will see that the answer is a grimace or an attitude of bewilderment.... we are not aware of our environments! We are not aware of how important it is in our lives to become aware of each of these environments to know how we move in each of them, how we feel, which ones make us happy, which ones affect us, which ones we control, which ones control us... only from this awareness can we, with effort and help, if necessary, modify our behavior in those environments that are not providing us with the stability we need to lead a full life and, at the same time, strengthen those environments that do have an impact on our development, evolution and happiness.

And you, do you know what are the environments in which you move? Or have you also grimaced in bewilderment?

According to Luis Gaviria, a pioneer in *neurocoaching*, there are ten winning environments:

#1 THE PHYSICAL. It refers to the environment, to the spaces in which we develop in our day to day, for example: home, work, gym, the park where we run, our office or any place where we develop some main activity in our daily life, such as the vehicle, for example, if we are drivers or commercial. Which must be adequate and optimized with the best conditions possible.

#2 SPIRITUAL: This environment does not refer to whether we practice any religion or if we believe in a God or Gods; as such it refers to our development and inner evolution, if we possess the qualities that make us beings who are living a full, happy, coherent and congruent life. A person who considers himself an atheist and yet is humble, delicate, educated, compassionate, has inner peace and gives love... is a spiritual person. It is about the construction of all that is considered the development of the interiority of a human being, who is capable of transcending, whether or not he or she practices a religion.

#3 THE SELF: It refers to our talents, values, character, abilities, skills, competencies, which exalt us and allow us to put them at the service and collaboration of others, in the same way it is part of this environment everything good and better that we want and expect from life... are we putting into practice the self to lead the life we want and deserve?

#4 RELATIONSHIPS: In this environment we find mainly the areas of close affective socialization, that is, with those with whom we lovingly and generously share our existence. It refers in particular to our family, our friends and our colleagues.

#5 SOCIAL NETWORKS: Here we have to understand social networks as the groups to which we belong and in which we can make a difference... these are the groups that we can call support groups because in them we can give and receive the help we often need. They are those key groups, people, entities, institutions or organizations that allow us to generate strong specialized links.

#6 BODY: This is an environment to which we must pay attention with much affection and dedication, because we are talking about our body, this temple that is accompanying us during our passage through this planet... to which we must take care with special dedication and give it all the help it needs in terms of food, exercise, wellness, contemplation, so that it can be our perfect vehicle while we are in the life cycle.

#7 MEMETIC: Here we are not referring to the so well-known funny memes that are going around the internet, no... here we refer to memes as cultural or behavioral elements that are transmitted from person to person and from generation to generation. As the scientist Richard Dawkins would say, "memes are learned or assimilated cultural units that are not genetically transferred". They are ideas, customs, practices, human referential elaborations that are powerfully transmitted from generation to generation and that instill a particular way of being. This environment teaches us to learn to live together and to grow in difference.

#8 FINANCES: This environment is obviously related to our economic income, and indeed includes the desire to have not only a higher income, but a much better one... although the beauty here is that this is an environment that well managed can bring great spiritual benefits if the increase of this income is not only destined to us, but also to sharing and helping. This environment motivates us to learn to lead our financial life in an orderly and prudent way so that it adjusts to the economic reality that we have, always with a view to making it better. It invites to plan, organize and project the procurement, use and investment of money.

#9 TECHNOLOGY: Here we refer to the means to which we have access through new technologies... they are the hardware, software and cybernetic environments that allow people to communicate and present themselves in the global village, this requires having equipment and learning how to use it. In particular, he alludes to the applications that facilitate two-way contact, with people or entities. He invites the use of social networks such as Twitter, Instagram, Facebook, Zoom, Skype. LinkedIn, Whatsapp, among others. These are tools that are offered to us for free and that well used we can turn them into environments of triumph.

#10 IMAGINATION: Thanks to imagination we have the greatest and best inventions, the most beautiful works of art, the most beautiful poems, the most tender stories... imagination allows us to survive the worst circumstances... imagination is an environment that can lead us to freedom inside a cell, this is turning the mind into a workshop of ideas.

Now that we know what we mean when we talk about environments of triumph, we must keep in mind that we are not alone in these environments and those around us will affect our environments, just as we can affect the environments of others... that is one of the reasons why we must be fully aware of the importance of our actions so that we can positively affect, with consciousness and feeling, all the environments in which we move, both our own and those of others.

Likewise, we must know and be fully aware of the great importance of knowing how to direct our thoughts and actions in order to responsibly choose our environments, because our success and happiness will depend on this choice; we must develop the character and maturity necessary to choose with common sense, self-confidence, security and freedom what kind of person I choose to be, what are the values that represent me, where I want to live, how I want to live, what I want to study, where I want to work, whom I want to marry, how I want to educate my children, what financial situation best suits me, etc.

And of all the environments we have mentioned, there is one to which we have to pay special attention... that does not mean that we can neglect the others... no!... I just want to emphasize the importance of being very careful with our environment of imagination... it is very powerful! If you pay attention, messages are permanently coming to us, with different words and by different means, emphasizing that "what you focus on expands", or "where you put your attention, you put your energy", or "you are the creator of your reality"... and all this starts in the imagination, which just as it can open the most beautiful reality and give you the most prosperous future... it can also become your main opponent and main stumbling block. I am not going to dwell on examples because it is enough to give you an idea so that you know what I mean... if your partner, or your child, or any relative you are waiting for does not arrive at the agreed time, doesn't your imagination fly to the worst possible circumstances to explain that delay... or if you are waiting for the call to confirm that you have been accepted in a new job, which you also need, it is noon and you still have not been called... don't you start to despair believing that you have not been accepted when there is still a long day ahead of you?

We must be extremely careful with our environment of imagination, have the ability to turn it into our environment of triumph par excellence and for this we must use good judgment, something that distinguishes us as human beings and conscious beings. We must have the good judgment to rationalize in order to understand that our thoughts generate our feelings/emotions and these feelings/emotions generate our behaviors... our DOING.

I'm sure you've already realized this, however, let's put it into words: our imagination environment is so important that it affects each of the other nine other environments... imagination is our best tool and we have the right to use it, as well as the duty to take care of it.

Now that we know the importance of our behavior, of our DOING, knowing that this is based on a cognitive process in which we have the responsibility to direct, we have more than enough reasons to return to the subject of our book... golf.

In the previous chapter we dealt with the subject of self-leadership, which is the attitude we must take to decide what we want our ideal winning environments to be like and the ability to turn each of them into the chosen winning environments. These will be our environments, where we will be able to fulfill ourselves and achieve excellence as human beings, environments where we will be able to be fulfilled and happy, to be able to share and teach all those who are related to each of our environments.

From this particular topic of imagination, which is basic and fundamental for our development as human beings in order to achieve personal fulfillment, we realize the deep connection it has with golf, because its foundations help us to enhance our ingenuity, which gives us the ability to invent and solve problems by finding the right means, to bring to reality our reflections or make real the non-existent, since imagination is to represent in our minds something that does not exist or is not present.

So, we need to activate our ingenuity to make our imagination our best ally, always from the light, silencing the dark side and to achieve this golf gives us a wide range of tools and fundamentals to develop physical, emotional and psychological capabilities that we need to generate strategies that lead us to achieve this important goal of acting with ingenuity to change our lives and the lives of those around us.

The truth is that creative strategy is like golf, because whoever wants to be a good golfer, what he does is to repeat his swing countless times following his preparation routine, in addition, before hitting the ball he will consider absolutely all possible variables and decide which is the appropriate club for the shot he wants to achieve... it is all a strategic creative process. Every shot, no matter how much it resembles another, the same course, no matter how many times he repeats it in the game, will be different, not only because everything changes day by day, but in particular because the golfer adds his own ingenuity to every shot, which makes it always new and different.

Good ideas do not come out of nowhere, in fact, good ideas are based on key and basic techniques and information, on time and patience, on resources that allow the freedom to study different actions, to explore new concepts and even take risks to improve results... yes! you must also know how to optimize the tools and resources available, for this it is important to make a good planning, seek and obtain more and better information that gives us the basis to propose different and creative solutions that produce performance. All this is achieved with imagination, particularly with ingenuity.

And obviously, once our game or our project is over, we will have to measure the results to locate the mistakes, what can be improved, the given conditions and thus, start again a new round or a new plan from the beginning... although planning is not easy, many of us agree that it is indeed necessary.

And so, when we have succeeded in leading our winning environments through self-leadership, then we are ready to lead others.

> Working in winning environments gave me clarity on what to study, where I wanted to work, who my friends would be, especially using imagination as a powerful tool.
>
> In addition to a friendly physical environment, we need supportive, human environments. For example, the quality of our relationships affects us greatly.
>
> Learning to design, create, modify and maintain our different environments is an art.
>
> — TESTIMONIAL FROM H.G.
> (ENTREPRENEUR WHO LEARNED
> GOLF IN HIS YOUTH)

> Through leading winning environments I learned to make good decisions such as: who to marry, the education we wanted for our children, the place where we would live, the people we would relate to, as well as the importance of knowing their cultures.
>
> — TESTIMONY OF J.E.
> (COLLABORATOR OF A COMPANY,
> WHO PARTICIPATES IN
> NETWORKING TOURNAMENTS)

My family and I thank Jorge for his wisdom in teaching us that there is a different way to live through the fundamentals of golf. He led us to find and design our winning environments on different levels: social, family, financial, spiritual, personal and professional.

Learning to connect or get in touch with people by making community allows us to navigate diversity and inclusion in their different generations.

— TESTIMONY OF W. R.
(COLLABORATOR IN A GOLF COURSE,
PRACTICES GOLF)

MENTAL CONCENTRATION EXERCISES:

#1 JUST ONE THOUGHT: from the numerous thoughts that visit your mind, choose one. It is preferable that it be a pleasant thought. Once chosen, dedicate yourself to give it all your attention, only to it. Try to be conscious of all the sensations produced by the fact of thinking only about the thought you have chosen. Try to intensify the pleasant sensations associated with that thought. Enjoy them. (Purpose: to put into practice the atmosphere of imagination).

#2 WALK WHILE COUNTING: walking improves concentration. If, in addition, when you are walking you do this little exercise, your concentration will increase: start counting five steps, at the next step start again, but count up to six. When you finish, start again and count to seven. Continue like this until you reach ten. Repeat the whole sequence during your walk. (Purpose: to practice the body's environment).

#3 ONE THING AT A TIME: as much as we are educated to be productive and multitask, we should stop doing it this way. When we attend to several things or thoughts at the same time, we lose a lot of concentration capacity. Mindfulness, which consists of paying full attention to what we are doing, is becoming more and more popular. If you are eating, just eat. If you are walking, just walk. In this way your attention will be trained and you will be able to transfer this ability to any activity. Therefore, when you start doing something, put all your attention only on what you are doing. The rest will have its time. (Purpose: to learn to overcome the resistances, this is the definition of everything that hinders any process of a winning environment).

ACTIVITIES DERIVED FROM THE CHAPTER:

1. Identify the environment that you consider you have developed and explain why.
2. Identify the environment that you have less developed and what prevents you from doing so.
3. Establish a relationship between each of the winning environments and golf.

7

LEADING OTHERS

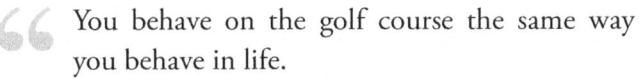 You behave on the golf course the same way you behave in life.

— F. CHIESA

BEFORE GOING INTO THIS CHAPTER, I WANT TO THINK about a quality that is absolutely necessary to be able to lead others, something that we must definitely **HAVE** as something inherent within us: coherence.

Coherence is being able to maintain a logical and consistent attitude with the beliefs or principles professed or practiced. Then, if our principles and actions are consistent, it will be not only possible, but also easy, to react with creativity, fluidity and intuition to any personal, social or work challenge.

And once again, golf is the sport that offers consistency as one of its main fundamentals, which is a quality that we can acquire or improve effortlessly and almost naturally with the practice of this sport that is based on respect for the opponent above the fact of losing or winning, where the rules are based on rules of courtesy and good manners that come to light even in defeat.

Now, returning to the subject of this chapter, let us remember that a leader is the one who influences others to work with attitude in pursuit of achieving the defined objectives, in addition, he is usually considered the boss. In practically all political, sports, religious organizations, etc., there is a leader, obviously, in each of these groups the leader will perform different functions, however, the best known and most widespread is the executive leader of business management and, in any case, the leader is the one who plans and directs the group, represents it and stands up for it, mediates in conflicts that may arise and knows how to promote, stimulate and encourage with sanctions and rewards.

There are different types of leadership for different groups and, obviously, depending also on the personality and ability of the leader we can have different types of leaders: authoritarian, who make decisions without consulting their team; democratic, who ask for and take into account the opinion of the group; and finally, liberal leaders, who decide only at the request of the team.

But before leading others, a leader must first be capable of self-leadership. Moreover, self-leadership is currently considered a basic habit for human beings since it is a great tool to give meaning and direction to life... think that the greatest leaders in the history of the world made their vision their very life... never their profession.

Now that we have the clear vision that a leader must have sufficient training to stay at the head of a team, we must be clear that a leader is obliged to, above all, have cultivated and covered a whole series of human qualities that allow him to stay in his position and achieve the personal development of each of the members of the team he leads, in addition to leading the team itself to achieve success in whatever the task undertaken.

Obviously, all the academic knowledge that a leader has, and all his or her human qualities, are not the product of a blossom, but rather the product of effort, combined, in most cases, with an innate charisma.

And all this knowledge and all these qualities are obtained and developed in the brain.

Currently we are working with the *brain-friendly* concept, closely related to *coaching*, social intelligence, *mindfulness* and *neuromanagement*, and refers to the way we manage our brain. It is known that born leaders have the ability to manage their brains more effectively than other people, that is, they have the genetic load that allows them to develop and train their brain more easily both physically, mentally and emotionally because, as Aristotle said, "excellence is not an act, but a habit"... so, with dedication and tenacity, we all have the ability to develop the skills needed to be leaders... better yet... to lead ourselves! and to be able to change for the better our future and that of those around us in our family, social and work environment as well, since, as we know, a leader has the quality of influencing others and are decisive in the progress of companies that are defined as successful ... because success is based on the base where the teams are, the workforce, which is where a leader has greater ability to influence.

We have already mentioned that every leader must possess a series of qualities and skills necessary to face and excel in this 21st century; these competencies must cover an important range that includes advanced technological knowledge, traditional managerial knowledge and soft skills that make him/her approachable and allow him/her to positively influence his/her team... and where can we develop all these requirements?... well, in the brain! And how? through the practice of healthy habits for the body - good nutrition, rest, exercise, etc. - and the mind - healthy thoughts, optimism, clear ideas - which will lead us, at the very least, to become tonic and non-toxic people... and how long will it take? That will depend on our perseverance and determination to break that initial resistance to change that our brain will present at first.

In short, the fact of cultivating the mind to make better use of it and cultivate all the human qualities that lead us to be better people, is the best way to lead ourselves and others, knowing that leading has nothing to do with imposing ideas or opinions, on the contrary, it is about listening and learning from those who know, with the intention of reaching something different leading with conviction, enthusiasm and optimism towards a common goal.

Let's clarify a little bit more our concept of leading, because maybe, right now you are wondering if leading is motivating, or maybe it is inspiring, or maybe it is obtaining results...

well, I think the best thing to do right now is to know the main qualities that every leader must **HAVE**[1] :

#1 FOCUS:

> It has been said that leadership is about making important but unpopular decisions. This is a partial truth, but it detracts from the importance of focus. To be a great leader, you can't focus on the little things and you must be less distracted than your competition. To attend to the critical things, you must develop some selective ignorance. Otherwise, the trivial will drown you out.
>
> — TIM FERRIS, BESTSELLING AUTHOR.

#2 CONFIDENCE:

> A leader gains followers and inspires confidence by having a clear vision, having empathy and being a good teacher. As a woman leader, I sometimes feel I must appear assertive without losing the generosity and kindness my parents taught me. Both of these characteristics help me gain respect.
>
> — BARRI RAFFERTY, CEO OF KETCHUM NORTH AMERICA

#3 TRANSPARENCY:

I have never liked the concept of wearing a "mask". As a leader, the only way to build trust with my team and colleagues is to be 100% authentic: open, flawed, but always passionate about our work. This has given me the freedom to always be present and consistent. They know what to expect from me.

— KERI POTTS, SENIOR DIRECTOR OF PUBLIC RELATIONS AT ESPN

#4 INTEGRITY:

Our employees are a direct reflection of the values we embody as leaders. If we are playing by the reactive and outdated rules of always wanting to be right, we limit the full potential of our business and lose quality talent. If you focus on being authentic in all your interactions, it will permeate your business culture.

— GUNNAR LOVELACE, CO-FOUNDER OF THRIVE MARKET

#5 INSPIRATION:

People always say I'm a self-made man. But there is no such thing. Leaders are not self-made; they are motivated by someone or something else. I came to America with no money or any belongings besides my gym bag, but I can't say I landed with nothing: some people gave me great inspiration and fantastic advice, and it was driven by my beliefs and an inner desire and passion. For that reason, I'm always willing to offer motivation to friends or strangers on Reddit. I know the power of inspiration, and if someone can use my experience to achieve greatness, I'm more than willing to help them.

— ARNOLD SCHWARZENEGGER,
FORMER GOVERNOR OF CALIFORNIA

#6 Passion:

You must love what you do. To be successful at something, you must become obsessed with it and let it consume you. No matter how successful you become in your business, you are never really satisfied and are always looking to make things bigger and better. You lead by example not because you think you can do it, but because it's the way you live.

— JOE PEREZ, CO-FOUNDER OF
TASTEAMDE

#7 Innovation:

In any system with limited resources and infinite population expansion - such as your business or the whole of humanity - innovation is essential not only for success, but for survival itself. Innovators are our leaders. You can't separate the two. Whether by thought, technology or organization, innovation is our only hope for solving challenges.

— AUBREY MARCUS, FOUNDER OF
ONNIT

#8 PATIENCE:

Patience is really the courage that comes from testing your commitment to your cause. The road to great things is always difficult, but the best leaders know when to abandon a cause and when to stay the course. If your vision is bold enough, there will be hundreds of reasons why your goal "can't be achieved" and you will face a lot of skeptics. Many things have to come together for a business to thrive such as competition, funding, consumer demand and always, a little bit of luck.

— DAN BRIAN, CEO OF WHIPCLIP

#9 STOICISM:

It's inevitable: we're going to find ourselves in some really fucked-up situations, whether they're costly mistakes, unexpected failures or unscrupulous enemies. Stoicism is, at its root, accepting and anticipating so we don't panic, react emotionally or aggravate things further. Training our mind, considering worst-case scenarios and regulating our unhelpful knee-jerk responses is how we keep these screwed-up situations from turning into fatal events.

— RYAN HOLIDAY, AUTHOR OF THE OBSTACLE IS THE WAY AND DIRECTOR OF MARKETING FOR AMERICAN APPAREL

#10 ANALYSIS:

Understanding the underlying numbers is the best thing I've done for my business. Because we have a subscription-based service, the biggest impact on our bottom line was lowering our attrition rate. Being able to reduce that number from 6 percent to 4 percent meant a 50 percent increase in the value of the average customer. Something I wouldn't have known how to do if I hadn't learned to understand my business data.

— SOL ORWELL, CO-FOUNDER EXAMINE.COM

#11 AUTHENTICITY:

It's true that imitation is one of the greatest forms of flattery, but not when it comes to leadership, and every great leader in my life, from Mike Tomlin to Scott Rawles' Olympic ski coach, has been authentic. It's okay to learn from others, read autobiographies of your favorite leaders and pick-up skills along the way, but never lose your voice and authentic opinions.

— JEREMY BLOOM, CO-FOUNDER
AND CEO OF INTEGRATE

#12 OPEN-MINDEDNESS:

One of the biggest myths is that good business leaders are visionaries who possess a steely determination to follow their goals no matter what. It doesn't make sense. The truth is that leaders have to keep an open mind and be flexible to adjust strategy if necessary. When you are in the startup phase, planning takes a back seat and your goals are not static; your objective should be to develop good relationships.

— DAYMOND JUAN, CEO OF SHARK
BRANDING AND FUBU

#13 DECISION-MAKING ABILITY:

In high school and college, to earn extra money I often refereed basketball games. The person who taught me how to do it gave me a great life lesson: "You have to make decisions fast, make decisions hard and don't look back". There are times when a bad decision well-made can give you better results in the long run and build a stronger team than the right choice made 'there and then'.

— SCOTT HOFFMAN, OWNER OF
FOLIO LITERARY MANAGEMENT

#14 BE GENUINE:

We all bring something unique to this world and we all notice when someone is not authentic. The more you focus on making genuine connections with people - beyond focusing on what they can do for you - the more likable you will be to others. This is not necessary to be a great leader, but it is necessary to be a more respected one, which can make a big difference in your business.

— LEWIS HOWES, AUTHOR OF THE
"MOST SALES" OR "MÁS YENDIDO",
WHICH IS LISTED ON THE NEW
YORK TIMES SCHOOL OF
GREATNESS LIST

#15 EMPOWERMENT:

Many of my leadership philosophies I learned as an athlete. My most effective teams don't always have the best talent, but they do have members with the right combination of skills and the ability to trust their teammates. To build a successful team you must delegate responsibility and authority, which is not always easy. That's the only way to discover the true capabilities of your people and get the best out of them.

— SHANNON PAPPAS, SENIOR VICE PRESIDENT, BEACHBODY LIVE

#16 Positivity:

To achieve greatness, you must create a culture of optimism. There will be many ups and downs, but the prevalence of positivity will help your company move forward. But remember: this takes courage. You must truly believe that your team can do the impossible.

— JASON HARRIS, CEO OF MEKANISM

#17 Generosity:

My biggest goal has always been to offer the best of myself. We all grow - as a collective, as a team - when I help others grow as individuals.

— CHRISTOPHER PERILLI, CEO OF PIXEL MOBB

#18 Persistence:

A great leader once told me "Persistence beats resistance". After working at Facebook, Intel and Microsoft to start my own company, I have learned two other great lessons: All things take time and you must persist, always. That's what makes you a good leader: the willingness to go beyond what would stop others.

— NOAH KAGAN, APPSUMO CEO

#19 Vision:

You need to use your instinct every day to know how to separate what is really important. It's like wisdom - it can be improved over time, but it must be part of you from the beginning. It's inherent. When your instinct is right, you look like a genius, but when it's wrong, you look like an idiot.

— RAJ BHAKTA, FOUNDER OF
WHISTLEPIG WHISKEY

#20 Communication:

If people don't know what your expectations are and don't meet them, it's really your fault for not communicating well. The people I work with are constantly talking. Communication is a balancing act. You may have a specific need, but it's imperative that you see the job as a collaborative effort.

— KIM KURLANCHIK RUSSEN,
PARTNER AT TAO GROUP

#21 ACCOUNTABILITY:

It's much easier to blame than to accept that you have some responsibility when something goes wrong. But if you want to know how to do things right, learn from financial expert Larry Robbins. He wrote a truly humble letter to his investors when a bad choice of his caused a profit loss. Then he opened a new fund with no account management fees or preferential fees - something never before seen in the industry. That's character. That's responsibility, that's going beyond accepting blame and doing something to remedy the mistake.

— SANDRA CARREON-JOHN, SENIOR
VICE PRESIDENT, M&C SAATCHI
SPORT & ENTERTAINMENT

#22 RESTLESSNESS:

It takes real leadership to find the strengths within each person on your team and then look outward to fill in what's missing. You have to believe that your team alone doesn't have all the answers, because if you come to believe that, it means you're not asking the right questions.

— NICK WOOLERY, DIRECTOR
GLOBAL DE MARKETING DE STANCE
SOCKS

"In short, the definition of leadership has nothing to do with hierarchy or anyone's position..., it has nothing to do with imposing opinions but with listening to those who know. Leadership is the **attitude assumed by those people who seek something different**, who are committed to achieving an objective and whose conviction they manage to transmit to others through enthusiasm and optimism, to achieve a common goal[2]".

It is now clear to us that the role of a leader is a role of utmost importance and necessity in all aspects of our lives, but it is also a role that implies a great responsibility and needs to **HAVE** a great physical, mental and emotional preparation and capacity... and golf, again, is one of the most complete sports that prepares us to assume this role. The physical aspect is, I think, pretty obvious, so let's look at just five of the many benefits that golf lends to our mental health[3]:

#1 REDUCES STRESS: According to *Golf Digest*, a 2015 study states that playing sports helps improve health, specifically outdoor sports, also known as "green exercise". In addition, they comment that experiences that allow greater contact with nature have been shown to reduce stress and mental fatigue.

Golf meets both of these characteristics, as it is an outdoor sport.

#2 DECREASES ANXIETY: According to a study conducted by more than 25 European doctors and international experts, golf contributes to improve the general health of people who practice it, and provides important benefits for mental health.

Roger Hawkes, former chief medical officer of the European Tour and one of the authors of the aforementioned study, explained in an interview conducted by CNN that social interaction is a risk factor that has been undervalued. While he expressed that "*moderate physical activity is associated with reduced anxiety and depression*".

#3 STIMULATES BRAIN DEVELOPMENT: According to Edwin Roald, a member of the European Institute of Golf Course Architects, golf acts as an excellent stimulator of the hippocampus - a brain region associated with memory, orientation and emotional regulation - one of only two areas of the adult brain where neurogenesis - the birth of new neurons - occurs.

Golf also helps to increase noradrenaline levels in the areas of the brain associated with cognitive activities - such as memory and decision-making - thus helping to improve our ability to learn.

Among other effects of neurogenesis on the brain is the increase in the feeling of well-being and cognitive abilities. Golf, as a good exercise, helps to raise serotonin levels, a key factor in people at risk of diseases such as Alzheimer's disease.

#4 PROMOTES SOCIAL INTERACTION: an article published by *Medical News Today* highlights the positive effects of social interaction for people. Psychologist Susan Pinker explains the physical benefit of interacting in an environment such as golf: "dopamine [is also] generated, which gives us some energy and decreases pain, it's like a naturally produced morphine".

In the article they expand on the importance of handshakes and physical interaction, however, due to the coronavirus pandemic we should avoid physical contact. Instead, we recommend you opt for a small bow or a *hi-five* from afar to acknowledge and thank your playing partner.

#5 REDUCES THE EFFECTS OF DEPRESSION: Surely, you've heard that exercising helps you produce endorphins, a hormone responsible for generating feelings of happiness, tranquility, euphoria and creativity. As mentioned above, there are several studies that prove that practicing sports such as golf can improve your mental state.

The constant practice of golf contributes to optimize the coordination and balance of the human body, stimulating neurological functioning and improving mental health.

In the golf trade magazine, ACES Northern California's Premier Golf Lifestyle Magazine, I have had the opportunity to read a series of articles that I can summarize as follows:

With golf we practice imagination, creativity, innovation and play; it also promotes concentration, focus, perseverance, thought control, tension management, confidence, preparation, balance, images and mental attitude... these are most of the qualities that a good leader needs to develop, and any person needs to be able to take responsibility for their goals, their wellbeing, their evolution... their life!

In addition, golf brings us fundamental values such as respect, honesty, perseverance, commitment, cooperation and exemplarity. These are attitudes that make us better people, employees, bosses and managers, and above all make us aware that "you cannot be a better boss than a person".

But golf goes beyond the individual, it even reaches the business aspect considering that it promotes the training of management skills such as the ability to visualize different scenarios, relying on mental toughness, control of emotions and self-confidence.

As you can see, although there is a widespread belief that leaders are "born", the truth is that they are also "made"... what's more, be sure that a born leader is a person who strives every day, prepares, searches, learns, invents, reinvents, strives... and, above all, knows how to be grateful, is a humble person in his greatness who knows how to give back to life all that life offers him.

 It is said that a good leader has the ability to enhance the skills of each member of his team. You have to be an example to follow, when you generate confidence in people allowing them to make mistakes, they develop their maximum potential, the same thing happens in golf when we make a mistake allows us to recover in the next shot but not without having learned from the mistake.

" I used to be a boss who forced situations to get the job done on time and on budget regardless of what my collaborators needed. However, after learning the basics of golf and putting into practice what I learned, I realized that I can get more out of my employees if I take the time to get to know each one as a person, as well as the talent they have, I learned that I can get better results by delegating with responsibility and trust. I invite different organizations to consider this excellent golf fundamentals program that taught me that before being a good leader you must first be a good person.

" Through the fundamentals of golf I learned, first, to know myself and recognize that I am in charge of my life and the situations I can control; secondly, having designed my winning environments gave me the basis for the right choice of my collaborators, the right pressure to exert, the release of talent, the positioning of objectives, enjoyment, confidence, coherence, concentration and balance to lead teams;

thirdly, the importance of active listening in communication for decision making and negotiation; fourthly, understanding that fostering social and professional relationships allows us to make better and healthier businesses and fifthly, making me an eternal learner through continuous education.

— TESTIMONIAL FROM F. L. (DIRECTOR OF A COMPANY THAT PRACTICES GOLF)

MENTAL CONCENTRATION EXERCISES:

#1 ORGANIZATION WHEN STARTING: when beginning any task, whatever type it may be, it is very important to have a minimum of organization. On the one hand, it will be necessary to avoid that the place where we are going to be has things that can distract us. The best thing is that it is a quiet and tidy place. The door should be closed, all Internet distractions should be turned off and the cell phone should be turned off. Also, write down what tasks you are going to do and in what order you will carry them out. In this way, by having a certain structure, concentration will be favored. (Purpose: to recognize that a leader applies the environments of triumph and leadership to their different tasks).

#2 A MOMENT OF MINDFULNESS: this exercise can be done at any free moment you have throughout the day. Waiting for the bus or during a break at work. Focus as much as you can on your breathing for two minutes. You should be standing with your eyes open and your breathing should be abdominal. All your attention will be focused on the sound of the air coming out of your nose and the rhythm of that breath. Thoughts will come to you that you should not attend to. When this happens, return your attention to the breath. If you do this simple exercise in moments of confusion or distress, you will see how it brings you tranquility and clarity of ideas. (Purpose: To recognize that a leader learns from golf and teaches leadership from golf).

#3 START WITH RELAXATION: our ability to concentrate is greatly diminished by the states of stress and anxiety with which so many people live. The ideal would be to acquire the habit of beginning each day with a meditation. This would bring us greater serenity for the rest of the day. If, in addition to this, we do small relaxations throughout the day and before starting any task, the level of concentration will be much higher. Start by taking several deep breaths. Breathe in through your nose and out through your mouth. Hold the air in and out for several seconds. Imagine all your tensions leaving as you breathe out. Repeat several times and then breathe in through your nose slowly, but without holding your breath. Now you will be much calmer and your breathing will keep you calm. (Purpose: to recognize that a leader is prepared to keep calm in a work team and is resilient).

ACTIVITIES DERIVED FROM THE CHAPTER:

1. Which of the qualities of a leader do you identify with and why?
2. Write a short piece of writing in which you can relate one of the benefits of golf to leadership.
3. Create your own leader slogan.

8

LEADERSHIP OPPORTUNITIES

 Golf as a sport is a lesson in humility

— PETER UIHLEIN

WHEN WE TALK ABOUT LEADING OPPORTUNITIES, WE are referring to the opportunity we are offered to take the initiative and share our knowledge to become creators of possibilities that allow others to move forward in life by developing their capabilities, attitudes and aptitudes. This has to be an opportunity chosen and assumed with awareness and emotion, because, although the supreme goal is to share and GIVE BACK with kindness and detachment all the benefits that we ourselves have been able to obtain thanks to the constant practice of golf, the truth is that we will continue to obtain rewards from this kind practice... this is how it has to be assumed with total responsibility and as a permanent act of retribution. This is as a leader I keep receiving and I keep giving back. We can find different studies that show that the key to achieve happiness, the supreme goal of the human being, is to share, not only time and goods, but also knowledge. And not only benefits the person who receives the knowledge that is being shared, in fact, generosity strengthens the relationships between the members of a community because it enriches the lives of its members. In this way, everyone benefits.

When a person shares knowledge, as we have said before, he is also rewarded because he broadens his horizons -you learn from those you teach-, he stays motivated -the interaction can acquire new good habits- and it gives purpose to his life -there is nothing more beautiful than seeing a life transformed-.

Throughout this book we have talked about the benefits that golf brings to people's lives on a daily basis, how it benefits companies and their people, and finally, we have also mentioned how it helps us prepare for the new skills needed in a world based on new technologies... but the truth is, I don't think these new skills are confined to the golf course, I believe that these new skills are not limited to the work area but include our daily life in which, more and more, and practically everything, is automated... and yes, in all aspects of our lives, even being so digitized, we can use golf, what it brings and teaches us to our advantage, sharing the benefits and what we learn with people, in companies and networks. Golf makes human beings continue in contact and closeness, as opposed to the coldness and absence generated when excessive use is made of cyberspace.

Therefore, sharing and participating in the knowledge of a company brings us a series of measurable benefits in addition to directly benefiting the active participation and happiness of workers:

- Develops a competitive advantage by promoting innovation and creativity by maintaining the flow of information.
- Improves productivity and performance, as well as progress towards a mission or objective.
- Information is shared throughout the organization.
- Redundant and unnecessary work is removed.
- Stimulates creativity, which leads to learning new things.
- Strengthens the bonds between people.

Nowadays we live in an era in which time is, precisely, one of the scarcest resources, everything moves with immediate speed; the fact that a leader has credibility and is recognized, strengthens the informal channels that help information flow in teams and in the company, allowing the participation of all team members and also between different teams.

Now, when we talk about new technologies in which, generally, relationships are carried out on virtual platforms, is there a place for sharing information? of course there is! Of course it does! because as human beings, we are willing to collaborate with each other and in situations like the ones we are currently living, where sensitivity is at the surface, is when we must show our human quality sharing -for free- what we are experts in, what differentiates us and allows us to be unique in our business niche... and yes, virtual platforms are there for that, and believe me, that "free" is relative, because we will also get benefits in terms of trust and authority in the sector in which we move, we will attract a community around what we are sharing, we will influence our industry and we will become known, in addition, we will have the great opportunity to learn and signify ourselves, not only because we can share information and knowledge, but also because we will be forced to do so to stay in the market ... it will serve as an incentive. Because when we teach we also learn, and to a greater extent.

We should not be afraid of technology; on the contrary, it is allowing information to flow, to arrive, to be shared, to be updated... to move! How many times have we heard that he who holds the information holds the power... well, that is changing thanks to technology, today we can begin to say and believe that in reality "power is shared knowledge".

As the great objective of golf is precisely to share and make known the great benefits that this magnificent sport is able to bring, there are more and more organizations in the world that are dedicated to promoting it, in many cases non-profit, such as the First Tee of Fort Worth, whose mission is to impact the lives of young people under the age of eighteen by providing them with the opportunity to participate in a life skills and core values curriculum through golf, instilling values that enhance life, foster leadership, build character, promote community service and promote wellness. This organization works with volunteers who, making merit to the sport they are dedicated to, are a positive role model of behavior, maturity and responsibility for the participants.

We have given as an example First Tee, which is aimed at children and young people, however, since golf is a sport that has no barriers, anyone who wishes to do so, will have no obstacle or problem finding an organization in their region where they can get started in this sport and enjoy the countless and lasting benefits of golf.

> The book Your Best Shot changed my vision of leadership, I had a very wrong reference of what it was to lead, probably because I believed that to be a good manager was to be a great leader. Now I not only want to inspire to achieve results in the organization, I want to inspire profound changes in the way we see life and above all in our role as citizens of the world. This has been the most challenging element and is generating important changes in the way I work with my teams.
>
> — TESTIMONIAL FROM C.T. (AN INTERNATIONAL BUSINESS MANAGER, GOLF PRACTITIONER)

> Volunteering has given me the opportunity to connect and share with people from different parts of the world, understanding each other through the language of golf, values and life, social, professional and managerial skills.
>
> — TESTIMONY OF L.A. (RETIRED FROM A TRANSNATIONAL COMPANY, VOLUNTEER AT THE FIRST TEE)

> Knowing golf has taken me to different places in the world and has allowed me to enjoy

nature, flora and fauna, to see the care and respect for the environment, and to see the job opportunities that are presented in this industry, as well as the economic and leisure impact it generates worldwide.

Now I have the opportunity to share all the knowledge, values and skills that I can apply in my life and that I have acquired through the fundamentals of golf and my performance as a volunteer in different organizations that teach the technique and qualities of golf.

— TESTIMONIAL FROM A. H. (WIFE
OF BUSINESSMAN WHO LEARNED
GOLF TO PLAY IT WITH HER
PARTNER ON BUSINESS TRIPS)

MENTAL CONCENTRATION EXERCISES:

#1 IN YOUR MIND VISUALIZE THE COLOR YOU WANT, hold the image of it for 40 or 50 seconds. The important thing is that you increase the time to visualize the color in your mind, you will see that, in a very short time, you will be able to stay very well concentrated for hours. (Purpose: To learn to visualize what you have learned about golf that you can share with others).

#2 WHEN YOU ARE READING A MAGAZINE OR A BOOK, stop on the image that catches your attention, and observe it for 2 or 3 minutes. After you have observed it, think of 23 adjectives that perfectly qualify the image you observed. You can write them down or record them in your mind. (Purpose: to keep in your memory the best moments of your golf practice.

#3 TAKE A BOOK, OPEN IT ANYWHERE, and start counting the words in each paragraph, long or short. When you think you have counted the words on a page, I invite you to write down the result, and count again to confirm if you did it right. (Purpose: to recognize that practice makes perfect).

ACTIVITIES DERIVED FROM THE CHAPTER:

1. List a knowledge, skill, or technique that you know well and could teach to others.
2. Recall an experience in your life in which a teaching positively transformed your life, briefly describe it.
3. Cut out and paste a picture of a person you consider to be a life teacher.

9

FOOTPRINTS THAT LEAVE A MARK

 May no one ever come near you, without leaving feeling a little better and happier!

— MOTHER TERESA OF CALCUTTA

HAVE YOU EVER THOUGHT OR WONDERED HOW WE walk, do you realize that we are not aware of the steps we take, or even how we support or place our foot?

Let's use our imagination, let's take a walk on a golf course... let's imagine ourselves walking on the course, stepping on the green and lush grass... when walking, we start the movement of the foot by supporting the rear foot or heel, then we support the arch and finally the forefoot or toe... this last part of the process of taking a step is the "shuttle" to take the next one. While walking, can anyone keep both feet in the air at the same time, can't they, because what happens is that in order to walk, we need a minimum of stability, balance, firmness and security at all times.

With each step we exert pressure with our foot, and depending on the terrain we leave an imprint, or what is the same... we leave a footprint.

Most of us mortals, unless we are dancers, start at the heel. In my personal case, the foundations of my footprints are values and principles, and on these are based all the other phases of my step to make the path... we are so automated in the walk that we forget the path.

The "footprints that leave a mark" are consolidated and maintained over time when their structure is based on non-negotiable and indelible values and principles that dignify human beings and lead them towards excellence.

We all have a story and anyone could be here, in my place, writing and sharing their story. If in my story there is something that you identify with, something that moves you or something that confronts you, and if you even come to think: "Jorge Croda is not talking about him, but about me", then I will have achieved part of my life's purpose: **to inspire**.

That is my wish with this book, to inspire from my life story that begins long ago, begins with my ancestors, and will not end soon, not even with my grandchildren... because we all live long before our birth and long after our departure... that is why the traces are so important, both those that our ancestors have left to us and those that we will leave to our descendants.

I am Jorge Croda. I have been happily married to Linda for 30 years and together we have three wonderful children, María Jimena, 29, who just made us grandparents of our granddaughter Camila, and Jorge and María José, who are 26 and twins. I currently work as an industrial engineer, superintendent in the golf industry and *coach*.

My extensive experience of more than 20 years as an entrepreneur and golf player and coach in Latin America, Europe and the United States has led me to inspire and help both individuals and companies to achieve their goals, embarking on the path of transformation and leadership based on respect, love, trust, teamwork and accompaniment.

Today I choose to share with you part of my life experience. A life that has been built and has made its way step by step on my identity based on values and principles, that is: "who I am, before what I do".

The different terrains on which I began to take my first steps helped me to strengthen my feet, as the terrain we walk on can help or hinder walking.

Since my origins, I have walked through lands in which humility, effort, commitment, dedication and a great capacity for resilience were very present. Most of these virtues were projected in me thanks to the example of my family, especially my grandfather.

My **BEING** has been transformed step by step, and in each one of them I have had the fortune to leave my mark, which has undoubtedly led me to define my life purpose: "To inspire human beings to develop as authentic leaders of exceptional value" ... and today I have the privilege of being able to fulfill that dream (to inspire) from one of my passions: golf.

Why golf? Because golf is a living example of life. Because there is an intimate relationship between what we need to play and what we need to live; because golf builds character, strengthens identity and shapes personality.

One of the biggest barriers that athletes and human beings encounter, and that must be overcome in order to achieve their goals, is the barrier of the mind, limiting beliefs and unresolved frustrating experiences.

Golf has been and is the perfect place to exercise the muscles of my personality, it is my personal emotional gym and the best school to develop the different subjects that life presents me, and all these opportunities that it gives me, it can give them to you and to anyone who wants to get started in the, believe it or not, exciting world of golf.

Each obstacle on the golf course, each distance, each meter, each hole, each lost ball, each chosen club and each posture, have become building blocks, analogies whose reflection have opened doors for my life.

Thanks to golf I have been able to polish my identity, what I am, live, transmit and express. In coherence of thought, word and action. It is my second skin, my third lung, the expression of my whole being. Thanks to golf I have reached fulfillment in life, I am happy, with a deep sense of humility and gratitude I can feel worthy of prosperity and well-being, but, above all, I feel the imperious need to share all this knowledge and all these feelings.

I have a lot to thank my ancestors, their footsteps, which preceded mine and softened my path, and golf for giving me the possibility to open my mind and heart to have the vision and sensitivity to understand this truth.

To conclude this book, which I hope will serve as a guide for you to build a full, fruitful and happy life in all your environments, I want to leave you a small summary of how my steps are... I invite you to join me, I offer you my experience as a support to achieve your goals and solve your concerns:

I START WALKING, I support the heel, which represents my pillars, values and principles.

I continue to build the foundation of my life on the pillars of the history of my ancestors, on their tradition, beliefs, faith, values, customs and culture, which are firm columns founded on love.

With joy, I see that today the child whose family showed him a path on which shoes are worn is still alive in me. My foot has grown and developed, especially because I have put myself many times in the other's shoes. My grandfather's maternal sensitivity and passionate stories are still alive in me. A family based on values remains in time: authenticity, solidarity, responsibility, fidelity, gratitude, kindness, freedom, justice and industriousness.

I REAFFIRM MY STEP, support the whole arc, and clarify the vision, mission and purpose of my life.

I define the path to follow because: "he who does not know where he is going, ends up anywhere". I establish a north that I am willing to travel with commitment, responsibility and total coherence; this is what is called strategic planning.

In other words, it is time to clearly know the purpose of my existence in this world... and I know it: "to accompany others to rediscover their greatness", knowing that together we will overcome paradigms, resistances, fears, limitations, bad habits, fears and uncertainty, which are the situations that block and stagnate the growth and development of people and organizations.

I FINISH THE STEP, support the tip and get ready for the next step... the action.

At this point we move from formation to transformative action; it is when seeds sown in the right soil and cared for with the right care bear fruit.

It is valid to clarify that the above topics are not always easy to explain, and my job as a *coach*, from the commitment and professionalism, is to help you to understand and internalize them, accompanying you to be and exploring learning methodologies based on *coaching* and its tools, neurosciences and communication skills, in addition to making use, if necessary, of other methodologies that also add and contribute to "accompany people to find their greatness" and "make leadership teams "high performance teams"".

MY FINAL MESSAGE

I INVITE YOU TO STAND UP AND BECOME AWARE THAT you have the capacity to make decisions, to take steps towards action, a transforming action based on values.

I invite you to look to the future from that position of firmness, security and stability on your two feet, with the deep desire to leave your mark with your training, style and personality.

Here is a gift I want to give you: four elements that support your footprint, SAFE:

- Recover the "**BE**" to execute with more intelligence and wisdom the steps that bring us closer to our purposes.
- Remember that the game is played by you. Yours are the steps that lead you to victory, yours is the **Self-leadership**.
- Project yourself into the **future** remembering your origins, living the present with intensity, emotion,

passion and strength, starting from who you are and developing that great potential that exists in the human being.

- Remember that many of the limits are created by our fears and that **Training** can break those barriers.

Ah... one more thing: **you are not alone!**

No, you are not alone... we have already mentioned in this book that there are organizations and many clubs that offer introductory golf programs within the reach of virtually everyone, and there are even many free introductory golf programs.

But golf is more than a simple sport, because above all it is a coherent sport, and those of us who participate in the spirit of this sport and are based on its fundamentals believe in the goodness of the human being as a pillar of society.

My family and I can attest to all the benefits of this sport in all areas of our lives. We are living the benefits offered by the practice of golf and we recognize that we are grateful to it. My children Jimena and Jorge practiced this sport at an amateur level and from a very young age, thanks to this, they had the opportunity to travel and participate in different competitions, which gave them the opportunity to meet and interact with people who throughout their lives have given them opportunities at a personal and professional level; they even had the opportunity to access scholarships that obviously were of great help to them and to us, their parents. My daughter María José never played at an amateur level, only socially, however, thanks to the fact that she never stops playing golf, she had the opportunity to teach this game to her boss, which allowed her to create a very special bond both with him and with the company where she works, since the innumerable qualities, basically moral, that are cultivated in golf came to light; and let's not talk about her circle of friends, she is always willing to lend a hand and teach golf to anyone who is willing to live this magnificent experience. And today that our family has been blessed with the arrival of Camila, my granddaughter, we see how the patience, tolerance, flexibility and serenity acquired by her parents thanks to the practice of golf (my daughter Jimena taught her husband, Camila's father, to play golf) create the right environment for Camila's development... she is an incredibly quiet, peaceful and calm baby.

So, it's good to know that in the United States and around the world you can find organizations, such as First Tee, which is a youth development organization that impacts the lives of young people by providing educational programs that build character and instill life-enhancing values through the game of golf. First Tee was founded by the World Golf Foundation, whose mission is to unite the golf industry around initiatives that promote, enhance growth and provide access to the game worldwide, while preserving the traditional values of golf and passing them on to others.

As you can see... you are not alone!

I emphasize this because it is very important for you to know that you are important... we all are! This is a universal truth that very few of us manage to make it our own and live it to the fullest; we have to be sincere and accept that it is not easy to reach that state in which **we feel** the magnitude of our importance... although that is why we are here and now, because we are perfect for this moment, we are neither lacking nor surplus... this is our moment!

I am so convinced that **it is important to know how important we are**, that I have made this phrase the title of the first chapter of my next book, in which I myself, in coherence with my life, my feelings and my knowledge, accompany those who wish to achieve fulfillment in their lives based on the fundamentals of golf... obviously I will recommend that you include the practice of this sport, because the fact of offering your mind a good physical and emotional state that accompanies and complements its development, is a gift for your life and for those who share it with you.

While you have had this book in your hands and have walked through its lines, our lives have walked together... I hope we can continue together for a few more days during my next book in which I share my life and the basis of my **GROW** service *coaching* program, which is based on the fundamentals of golf and is aimed at anyone, without any conditioning, who wishes to live the advantages that this sport gives us.

ANNEX I

This attachment is to give you a short scope of what is the GROW program, with which I work as a coach and consultant. Through this program I serve people, golf courses and organizations, evaluating and accompanying them to evolve from what I have learned in the past and in the present to create a positive and sustainable future.

At GROW we seek to be better people by trusting our intuition and making life as it should be... enjoyable! Knowing that the path to decision making can be precise, like a golf shot.

Just like a 9-hole course, here are 9 fundamentals that are deepened in the program and that serve as a starting point to reach the state of life that each one of us desires:

- Imagination: What do I want to achieve? (Big box).
- Curiosity: What are the possibilities?
- Visualization: How can I get there? (use your creativity).

- Strengths: How can I use my talents to achieve my goal?
- Attitude: To have balance and equilibrium, to be positive.
- Adapt: Be prepared for any situation.
- Focus: Being present in the moment.
- Flow: Timing is everything.
- Perseverance: Align with the objective and follow through.

Moreover, all this in a calm and relaxed way... without focusing on results, but on doing the best we can based on:

- Safety first.
- Be kind to others.
- Give each task to the best of your ability.
- If you make a mistake, tell someone.
- Have fun and enjoy your work.

I believe that the following tips will help you to get a clearer and closer idea of the values that golf can instill in you and that, with the GROW program, we manage to develop, enhance and internalize them. These tips are some of the codes or rules of dress and behavior that you should contemplate if one day you are invited to play a game of golf, if you decide to practice it as a hobby or if you want to dedicate yourself to this sport in a social way, it doesn't matter, you should always comply with them... just like life is!

Nine practices to keep in mind if you are invited to play golf:

1. Try to dress appropriately, the most recommended are chinos and a polo shirt, always accompanied by shoes designed exclusively for playing golf.
2. Have the necessary equipment and accessories for the game of golf.
3. Arrive at least 30 minutes before tee time at the golf course.
4. Stretch before starting to practice making shots.
5. Demonstrate humility and wait for the person who invited you to the course to give you the instructions.
6. If you make a few bad shots, just say it will get better, I'm having fun.
7. Maintain codes of honor and respect on the course and with teammates.
8. Your body language speaks volumes about your personality.
9. Know the basic rules, if you are not sure of any decision, you can always consult a fellow player or your marker.

The following list are the mistakes you should avoid, because committing them will show that you are a person who does not pay attention to details, does not respect the game or teammates, which can mark you as someone unreliable and no one will want to play with you again, much less trust you... neither on or off the course:

Nine mistakes to avoid if you are invited to play golf:

1. Not arriving with the proper attire or with it without good grooming 2.

2. Showing up for the game without the proper equipment.
3. Not arriving on time for the start of the game.
4. Failure to warm up before the game
5. Assuming arrogant behavior towards the game and teammates.
6. Disowning and assuming rude or aggressive acts when you have bad shots.
7. Not respecting the codes of honor and behavior in the game and on the field.
8. Assuming inappropriate body language.
9. Misuse of basic rules.

The GROW program awaits you with great joy and professionalism to accompany you through the golf process.

ANNEX II

MORE THAN A GAME[1]

THE TRUE HISTORY OF GOLF

Golf, an important industry with a positive impact on America's economic, environmental and social agendas, continues to be misunderstood. **We are golf** is a coalition to tell the real story of golf. Not just the game, but the stories of the hardworking men and women who make it the greatest sport in the world, and whose livelihoods depend on it.

We are golf is a coalition of leading golf organizations including the Club Management Association of America (CMA), Golf Course Superintendents Association of America (GCSAA), National Golf Course Owners Association (NGCOA),, LPGA, PGA tour, PGA of America, USGA, US Golf Manufacturers Council, and the World Golf Foundation (NGF).....

Golf is a leading U.S. industry that makes a wide variety of positive contributions to our society...some of which are:

SUPPORT: Your contribution helps communicate all the charitable and fitness benefits of golf to congressional, executive branch and agency leaders.

Golf brings people together. Once you really see someone as a human being, it becomes impossible to ignore what they have to say and you might learn something. I think that's really important.

ALL ARE WELCOME: With many different ways to promote inclusion within the game of golf, **we are golf** supports various initiatives that grow the game through multiple channels. Golf is for everyone, and everyone interested in trying the sport should have the opportunity to play.

STARTING YOUR CAREER: Golf is a game for everyone. As a recreational activity for millions of people of all ages, genders and ethnic backgrounds, many people choose to pursue a career within the industry. **We are golf** seeks to facilitate access to the opportunities available in the world of golf.

GOLF CAREERS.

VARIOUS JOBS WITHIN THE GOLF INDUSTRY.

The golf industry has several job opportunities available along with internships. Positions on property may include: general manager, head golf professional, assistant golf professional, staff professional, course superintendent, assistant superintendent, caddy master, starters and groundskeepers, food and beverage managers, servers and more. Within the industry, positions may include: executive directors, marketing directors, presidents, executive vice presidents, executive vice presidents, executive directors, vice presidents, directors, managers and associates, to fill marketing, accounting, human resources, hospitality, legal and public relations positions.

INVITING EVERYONE.

Get golf ready is an affordable, industry-supported group lesson program that provides a welcome introduction to golf. It targets the millions of adults in the United States who have never played golf or have minimal experience in the game. You will undoubtedly develop your comfort and confidence and be able to go play this great game with family and friends.

The PGA Jr. Tour. League is a fun, social and inclusive opportunity for boys and girls under the age of 13 to learn and enjoy golf. Like other recreational league sports, participants wear numbered jerseys and play on teams with their friends. The program brings family and friends together for fun team golf experiences with expert coaching from PGA and LPGA professionals.

Drive, Chip and Putt championship, a joint initiative of the master tournament, the United States Golf Association and the PGA of America, is a free, nationwide youth competition that harnesses the creative and competitive spirit of girls and boys ages 7 to 15. Participants have the opportunity to compete for a spot in the national finals held at Augusta National Golf Club.

LPGA * USGA girls golf prepares juniors for a lifetime of enjoyment of the game and provides a solid foundation for girls who want to have fun with friends and family, compete in high school, college and/or local, state and national. Levels or to learn for future professional purposes, both inside and outside the golf industry. Empowers and inspires girls for the game of life.

Athletes of the World Foundation offers athletic scholarships for athletes, allowing them to continue their education through sports. Athletic spirit is defined by dedication, teamwork and integrity. Athletes of the World Foundation believes in these qualities. We believe in the athletes.

Kids Golf Foundation is a statewide youth golf association in Illinois that offers and supports various golf programs and events designed to introduce children between the ages of 5 and 17 to the sport of golf, its fundamentals, rules, history, etiquette, life lessons and more.

The USGA's **Play9 ™ Program** has been educating and rallying golfers and non-golfers alike around the concept of the 9-hole round as an important, yet simple, solution to address busy lives. Play9 is important to the game and your health as it promotes a time-friendly option.

The Sticks for Kids Program of the Golf Course Builders Association of America is dedicated to introducing and teaching young people about the game of golf. The program focuses on the idea that all children, regardless of socioeconomic status, should have the opportunity to play golf.

Footgolf is a combination of two popular sports: soccer and golf. The game is played with a regulation number 5 soccer ball on a golf course on shortened holes with 21-inch diameter cups located yards from the greens. Players adhere to the golf course dress code and do not wear soccer cleats.

Golf courses around the world   **Golf Around the World. - The R&A**

If you want to delve even deeper into the progress, evolution and advancement of golf, you can download a very interesting PDF document by simply searching the internet: **Golf Around the World. - The R&A**

ANNEX III

MY LIFE AND GOLF

I did not want to finish this book, my first book, without explaining why I am so passionate and grateful for golf.

For some reason, people are born with different qualities and attitudes that allow us to face each event of our lives in a different way, fortunately, I am a born optimist... and I say fortunately because otherwise, surely, I would not be here offering what I am at the service of anyone who wants and needs it through Croda Consulting.

I consider it appropriate to demonstrate with my own testimony from a biographical approach, that what is consigned in this book is not only theory, each of its chapters, reflections, teachings, bets, have a direct connection with my personal and family history. This work does not arise from an exclusive intellectual and theoretical intention, no, it is the product of the existing relationship between golf, leadership and coaching, with life itself, particularly my life.

Although I come from a lineage of hard-working, tenacious, fighting and kind people who came from Italy to carve out an abundant and honorable future in Mexico, I must admit that at some point all these qualities and values were lost, I and my siblings had to live a reality so different that we were even victims of violence.

However, my innate optimism and attitude -which can also be cultivated- allow me to be a clear example of strength and self-improvement. I have the gift and inspiration to turn evil into goodness, selfishness into generosity and hatred received into love given. My life has been a life of very hard stories and despite the cards I was dealt in it, I knew how to play them to create my own game of life.

Golf has been my life engine and my salvation to get here. I am a man of faith, fortunate, honest, generous, humble, fair, curious, disciplined, passionate, persevering and always grateful. What characterizes me is that I always give a frank smile and that I give what I have without expecting anything in return. They say that the one who gives the most is the one who receives the most, however, this is not my main incentive at all.

I admired my paternal grandfather who, having been orphaned at the age of eight, carved his own destiny and that of his family without knowing how to read or write. He became a well-respected farmer and rancher in the state where he lived, helped his mother raise his nine siblings. They were the children of Italian immigrants who came to teach and work farmland. The most important teaching I received from my grandfather is the phrase: "*To know how to command you must first know how to do things*," but I also learned from him to share knowledge and seek the opportunity to serve others. His passion was race horses, which I learned to ride when I went to his ranch to work as a farm hand to learn how to handle them; with the horses I was lucky enough to ride in several races, it was an indescribable experience full of adrenaline. Another important and determining lesson in my life was: "All relationships are based on trust".

God places special people throughout your life to take care of you. In my case it was Father Miguel, who taught me the value of spirituality and humility. Through Christian renewal and the Holy Spirit came to me the gifts that have accompanied me throughout my life and have saved me from various situations, above all, they have allowed me to be an instrument to help people to protect themselves from evil.

The most difficult stage of my childhood was when we were going through quite serious problems at home; at that time, my teacher Ramón Valdez Castellanos taught me to control and channel my emotions by teaching me to declaim, to play the mandolin and the marimba, skills that helped me to develop intuition, security and temperance when facing serious and dangerous situations.

Don Juan Cobo Rodriguez, my neighbor, taught me everything about the game and the world of golf, the value of family, and that there were other ways to live.

I admire Gary Player for his humility, I see myself reflected in him. Adversity made me stronger and more tenacious, I confirm that when you want to, you can, and like him, what moves me most is to help others. Coincidentally, we both share a passion for horses.

From my uncles-in-law on my mother's side, Humberto Cavallari (Italian) and Edwin Culp (American), I learned the values of perseverance, curiosity, creativity and innovation; they gave me the opportunity to believe that any idea, no matter how crazy or risky, was possible. They also taught me to manage opportunities from every problem and never accept a definitive no... Every no hides a yes as a possibility if you look for it.

My decision to go out to look for a different life, to be the person I wanted, took me to Monterrey, where I studied and graduated as an industrial engineer and administrator. Thanks to golf I was able to contact the owner of a construction company who gave me the opportunity to work there as a technical draftsman. As my career progressed, I worked in different industries such as glass, metal mechanics and agriculture and livestock.

I had the opportunity to work as an assistant to Dr. Sauma (former Navy SEAL) for a project in Ghana, Africa. With him I learned all about tropical crop research and development, leadership, teamwork, communication and discipline. My passion for agriculture, people, research and development of crops such as pineapple, led me to develop the CIACES technology center and the COVECA marketing company, which supported with the organization, training and training to transform the methods of cultivation, production and sale of products. Both centers introduced varieties and technologies for the cultivation and international sale of pineapple, but my best achievement was to achieve a substantial improvement in the lives of the communities involved.

Years later I had the honor of meeting Don Rafael Guillaumin, a visionary who at 70 years of age started a bamboo technology center, he kindly invited me to be part of the board of directors thanks to my background and knowledge; this project grew with excellent results and transformed forestry agriculture, permeating the most disadvantaged social classes in Mexico.

When I was thirty-six years old, life gave me a great jolt in my health, economy and existence...after many comings and goings of these trials that I experienced, I had the support of the president of the course where I used to play and he invited me to work at the club, because they had many problems with the maintenance of the course and also had to change and rebuild the grass of the *greens*. I was aware of the magnificent opportunity that life was putting in front of me and I asked for the opportunity to make a program that would involve, besides maintenance, cultural practices and training programs for those who wanted to start or improve in the practice of golf. The fact is that I developed a technological package with excellent results for the club. This was my start as golf course superintendent.

In a second setback of life, the violence in my country led me in agreement with my wife to move to another country and residence, for a short time while the storm passed, unfortunately it was not so, because the alternation between Mexico and the U.S. became increasingly complex and finally, we decided to settle in the United States.

After all that series of adverse events, I received an offer to work at Southern Oaks Golf Club to renovate it and put it up for sale. The owner of the club knew that I had the ability to achieve the impossible in a very short period of time, optimizing resources, talent, and using what I had at hand. I accepted this challenge and in just four months the course was sold at a price higher than the estimated value.

The new owner offered me to continue working on the field, which was subject to his expectations. He told me that the club was ranked 64th in the Metroplex, where there are more than 220 courses, and he wanted to position it among the top ten. I accepted the job and made a plan so that, with a reasonable budget and in a maximum of seven years, we would achieve the objective. In the end, I managed to position the Southern Oaks Golf & Tennis Club in second place in only five years and with an investment of only 70% of the budgeted amount.

From two of my great passions, people and golf, Croda Consulting was born with a mission, to create opportunities for individual, business and social growth through leadership development, using the values and principles of golf. The idea is that the consulting firm can work anywhere, with companies or groups of any size, from individuals to large teams, to help them reach their potential without creating dependency, offering services that are based on empowerment and creating independence that lead to results and long-term success. Since I am a person of principle, I base my calling on serving people through personal growth, character education, leadership development, organizational dynamics and the golf industry. I combine all of these multifaceted elements in my professional and personal relationships.

I am dedicated to teaching these values and life skills in all the environments in which I participate in order to create a better society, demonstrating that there are different ways to live, always becoming better individuals, children, siblings and friends. I wish to contribute to create environments where I can see my grandchildren be born, develop and live, with health, prosperity, security and freedom... environments with values and leadership, contributing to the community in what is necessary to achieve the world that I want to leave to my family as a legacy.

I am bilingual, innovative, astute and strategic. My motto is: "We are the architects of our own destiny". I believe that teaching others the importance of focusing on values in their personal and professional lives, the importance of social responsibility, are the key to creating a happier and more sustainable world. In addition, for my passion and service to the golf industry in general, in the country where golf is most practiced, I was named a Golf Ambassador, and also recognized within the top ten golf instructors in the U.S. and outstanding coach by First Tee. And for taking and transmitting the message to different parts of the world in the golf industry. I was also nominated for the Tällberg Foundation's Eliasson Global Leadership Prize for the fourth consecutive year.

The important thing is not what I did but how I did it. When I arrived in the U.S. I researched about the cameras that were available, I attended events to meet people, I got involved with The First Tee as a volunteer since by then I had my professional golf instructor credential and knew how to use the SNAG system, which was being introduced in schools, I also went to play in charity tournaments representing The First Tee as a coach with participants. I got to know the different cultures of the participants, the other coaches and the sponsors of the program. I became involved in schools in the most disadvantaged and troubled areas and was finally offered the opportunity to take courses to advance my certification as a coach in The First Tee curriculum. Since I could not legally work, everything I did was on a volunteer basis, which helped me prepare for the current moment. I met more than 65 golf courses in the Metroplex, where I offered my coaching services.

Little by little I became involved as a volunteer in the golf course superintendents associations of America, attending different committees at the local and national level; I also participated in representing them in Washington, Europe and South America. I interacted with the different golf entities sharing my knowledge on leadership, communication, teamwork, strategic planning, professional relations, management, budgeting, administration, etc. I finally got certified as a superintendent and from then on I wrote several related articles and published videos of jobs.

I use my professional and personal platforms to build and promote a culture of collaboration and community. I feel like a visionary both here in the United States and in my home country of Mexico. I am always willing to give back and volunteer my free time and work on life skills, because from experience I know how to overcome language and cultural barriers, how to connect and really enjoy interacting with anyone.

Today I am committed to making a better world, accompanying people to discover their purpose.

Finally, golf has given me friends with whom I have shared joys, successes, sadness and teachings that led me to the growth and formation of the human being that I am. The values acquired at home, those learned in golf, those contributed by my dear wife Linda, have led us to form a beautiful family with María Jimena, Jorge and María Jose.

For me, the value of family leads me to reflect on what I am, what I want for them, what I want for myself and what I want for my community. I gave myself the task of teaching my children this excellent formative sport that helped them to mold their character, gave them the opportunity to know themselves and the people with whom they interact, it is a key that will open many doors for them in the future because it is the sport that gives more contacts and also helps them in the way they relate to life itself.

SHAPING HOW YOU LIVE AND WORK THROUGH THE VALUES OF THE GAME OF GOLF.

Croda Consulting is dedicated to helping people and businesses be more successful.

Croda Consulting has over thirty-three years of multicultural experience in sports facility design and renovation, especially golf, soccer and baseball, process implementation and refinement, business optimization, human resources, employee training, team building and customer satisfaction.

Our team's versatile ownership and management experience with companies, businesses and industries, including complex processes and workforces, allows us to quickly recognize, evaluate and capitalize on opportunities in the marketplace. Our mission is to create opportunities for individual, business and societal growth through leadership development using the values and principles of golf.

I am the president of the company and responsible for multiple revitalizations of golf courses and sports fields that increased revenues and sustainability of the facilities, always managing to organize and lead the team of the most skilled and qualified professionals to help companies identify and meet their needs and objectives.

ABOUT THE AUTHOR
JORGE CRODA

 Jorge Croda, a native of Mexico, earned his bachelor's degree in industrial engineering from the Universidad Regiomontana. He is a passionate and experienced professional in the golf and agriculture industry, with more than twenty years of experience in Latin America, Europe and the United States. His experience as a player, coach, consultant, superintendent, industrial engineer and educator gives him a unique perspective on how to use life, business and social skills to his advantage.

He has founded Croda Consulting, where his expertise continues his mission to create opportunities for individual, business and social growth through leadership development using the values and principles of golf. With an innate entrepreneurial spirit, innovative thinking skills and his passion for golf, his area of expertise is to enhance the success of companies through the effectiveness of their leaders and teams by training and developing individuals and groups, emphasizing that he has extensive experience in leading multicultural teams.

He has proven worldwide success in golf course and sports course renovation, consulting, marketing, team building, creating optimal learning environments, leadership development and representing multinational companies.

He has served as superintendent in 2017 and was the first Hispanic to receive the nationally recognized TurfNet Superintendent of the Year Award in the US.

He is a First Tee Coach and is recognized among the top ten PGTAA golf teaching teachers.

His motto is "We are the architect of our own destiny" and he is convinced that teaching others the importance of focusing on values in their personal and professional lives, and the importance of social responsibility, is the key to creating a happier and more sustainable world.

Thanks to his constant learning, he has achieved certification as an ontological coach, NLP coach and neurocoach in safety, health and education.

His great purpose is to grow the game of golf for everyone.

ONE LAST THING...

Be sure that the book of the Law is always read in your worship. Study it day and night, and make sure that you obey everything written in it. Then you will be prosperous and successful.

(Joshua 1:8[1])

NOTES

2. LEARNING INTELLIGENCES AND NEUROSCIENCE

1. Didasc@lia Magazine: D&E. Cooperative publication between CEDUT- Las Tunas and CEdEG-Granma, CUBA.
   Vol. VII. Year 2016. Number 4, October-December
   https://dialnet.unirioja.es/descarga/articulo/6667026.pdf
2. https://www.elpais.com.co/opinion/columnistas/carlos-e-climent/las-similitudes-del-golf-y-la-vida.html

3. GOLF AND WORK

1. To learn a little about it I suggest this link: https://www.apd.es/que-es-el-entorno-vuca-y-como-afecta-a-la-supervivencia-de-las-empresas/

4. LEADERSHIP THROUGH GOLF

1. Maratea, Rafael (2011). "Leading with swing. Discover the art of leading through golf". Editorial Granica, Buenos Aires, Argentina, 2011.

7. LEADING OTHERS

1. https://www.entrepreneur.com/article/273183
2. https://www.game-learn.com/que-es-liderazgo-maneras-definirlo/
3. https://blog.santamariapanama.com/blog/golf-para-la-salud-mental#:~:text=Among%20other%20effects%20of%20it,suffer-ing%20from%20diseases%20such%20as%20Alzh%C3%A9imer's%20.

ANNEX II

1. Wearegolf. org

ONE LAST THING...

1. Recover from: https://biblehub.com/catholic/joshua/1-8.htm

Made in the USA
Monee, IL
22 March 2021

62656636R00095